KHANIQAHI-NIMATULLAHI
(CENTERS OF THE NIMATULLAHI SUFI ORDER)

306 West 11th Street
New York, New York 10014
Tel: 212-924-7739

4021 19th Avenue
San Francisco,
California 94132
Tel: 415-586-1313

4931 MacArthur Blvd. NW
Washington, D.C. 20007
Tel: 202-338-4757

84 Pembroke Street
Boston,
Massachusetts 02118
Tel: 617-536-0076

310 NE 57th Street
Seattle, Washington 98105
Tel: 206-527-5018

11019 Arleta Avenue
Mission Hills,
Los Angeles,
California 91345
Tel: 818-365-2226

4642 North Hermitage
Chicago, Illinois 60640
Tel: 312-561-1616

405 Greg Avenue
Santa Fe, New Mexico 87501
Tel: 505-983-8500

219 Chace Street
Santa Cruz, California 95060
Tel: 408-425-8454

95 Old Lansdowne Road
West Didsbury,
Manchester
M20 8N2, United Kingdom
Tel: 061-434-8857

Kölnerstrasse 176
5000 Köln 90 (Porz)
Federal Republic of Germany
Tel: 49-2203-15390

Van Blankenburgstraat 66b
2517 XS's-Gravenhage,
The Netherlands
Tel: 070-450251

50 Rue du 4em Zouaves
Rosny-sous-Bois
Paris 93110
France
Tel: 48552809

63 Boulevard Latrille
BP 1224 Abidjan,
CIDEX 1
Côte d'Ivoire
Tel. 225-410510

The Old Windmill
Sulgrave, Banbury,
Oxfordshire OX17 2SH
United Kingdom
Tel: 0295-760361

41 Chepstow Place
London W2 4TS
United Kingdom
Tel: 071-229-0769
Fax: 071-221-7025

JESUS
IN
THE EYES OF
THE SUFIS

Also available by Dr. Javad Nurbakhsh
1. *In the Tavern of Ruin: Seven Essays on Sufism*
2. *In the Paradise of the Sufis*
3. *What the Sufis Say*
4. *Masters of the Path*
5. *Divani Nurbakhsh: Sufi Poetry*
6. *Sufism (I): Meaning, Knowledge and Unity*
7. *Traditions of the Prophet*, Vol. I
8. *Sufism (II): Fear and Hope, Contraction and Expansion, Gathering and Dispersion, Intoxication and Sobriety, Annihilation and Subsistence*
9. *The Truths of Love: Sufi Poetry*
10. *Sufi Women*
11. *Traditions of the Prophet*, Vol. II
12. *Jesus in the Eyes of the Sufis*
13. *Spiritual Poverty in Sufism*
14. *Sufism III: Submission, Contentment, Absence, Presence, Intimacy, Awe, Tranquillity, Serenity, Fluctuation, Stability*
15. *Sufi Symbolism I: Parts of the Beloved's Body, Wine, Music, Sama and Convivial Gatherings*
16. *The Great Satan, 'Eblis'*
17. *Sufi Symbolism II: Love, Lover, Beloved.*
18. *Sufism IV: Repentance, Abstinence, Renunciation, Wariness, Humility, Humbleness, Sincerity, Constancy, Courtesy*
19. *Sufi Symbolism III: Religious Terminology*
20. *Dogs from the Sufi Point of View*
21. *Sufi Symbolism IV: The Natural World*
22. *Sufi Women: Revised Edition*
23. *Sufi symbolism V: Veils, Government, Medicine*

JESUS
IN
THE EYES OF
THE SUFIS

Jesus in the Eyes of The Sufis
By Dr. Javad Nurbakhsh
Translated by
Terry Graham, Leonard Lewisohn, and Hamid Mashkuri.
Cover design by Jane Lewisohn
Translators wish to express their gratitude for the
invaluable comments kindly provided by
Prof. Hermann Landolt.

First impression 1983
First reprint 1992

ISBN 0-933546-21-1

Published by Khaniqahi-Nimatullahi Publications — London
Printed in England

Address: 41 Chepstow Place
London W.2
Telephone: 01-229-0769

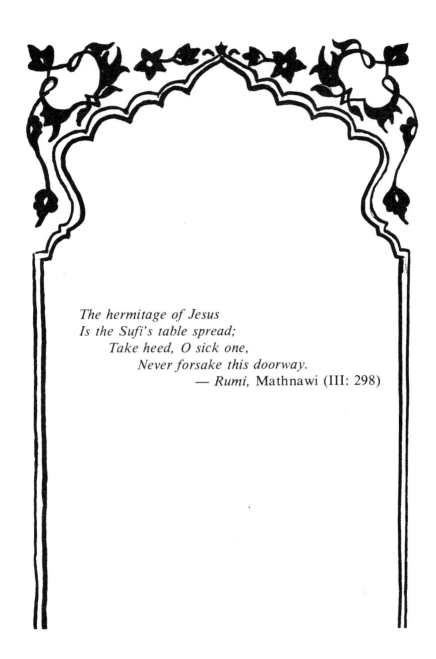

The hermitage of Jesus
Is the Sufi's table spread;
   Take heed, O sick one,
     Never forsake this doorway.
           — *Rumi*, Mathnawi (III: 298)

In the Name of the Transcendent, the Holy

Were the Holy Spirit to favour us once
More by its Grace, others too would
Perform all the works of Christ.

Ḥâfez

Jesus, as a Prophet of God, manifested the human qualities of sincerity, purity, love and charity. Despite the fact that the Prophet Mohammad always referred to him as a brother, and that the Qoran makes repeated mention of him with the highest praise, Moslem and Christian leaders have, for political reasons or out of sheer prejudice, forever striven to pass over this brotherly pledge and have it conveniently forgotten.

Only the Sufis, because of their lack of prejudice and their inner purity, have managed to avoid being influenced by what fanatical and extremist clerics have tried to inculcate. It is the Sufis who have attempted to preserve the memory of Jesus as he really was, alive in their minds, and in the minds of others, and to keep him in their hearts.

In Sufi literature, Jesus is the paragon of a perfect human being and the example *par excellence* of a true master. In fact, throughout the centuries, in all their 'Moslem-ness', the masters of Sufism, out of the purest sincerity and love, have had nothing but praise for Jesus, presenting him as a perfect Sufi.

A study of the writings of gnostics and Sufis reveals how Jesus invariably appears as a perfected master in anecdotes and instructive discourses; and scarcely a Sufi poet can be found who has failed to cite Jesus in his verse.

This profound consideration which the Sufis have for Jesus has prompted me to make a more thoroughgoing study of the Sufi gnostic works, with a view to making my findings available to devotees and all who might be interested. My research has been somewhat hampered by the fact that I am currently residing in the United States, where I have not had access to all the possible materials; however, I have done my best to put together something which would make Moslems think more about Jesus, while stimulating Christians to take a closer look at Islam and not place all Moslems in the same category, by being conscious of the fact that Sufism, from the doctrinal point of view, owes a great deal to Jesus, as well as in actual practice, where Jesus's spirit has always prevailed in Sufi ethics and behaviour.

God alone is eternal,

Dr. Javad Nurbakhsh
5th April 1982
16 Farvardin 1361

CONTENTS

TRANSLITERATION EQUIVALENTS

Arabic Alphabet	Latin Alphabetic Equivalents	Pronounciation of Unfamiliar Sounds

Consonants

Glottal stop, as at the beginning of any English word which starts with a vowel

أ ع ,

ب b

ت t   th   As in 'think' — unvoiced (Arabic); simply s in Persian

ث th

ج j   kh   Guttural as German or Scottish **ch**

ح ḥ

خ kh   dh   As in 'the' — voiced (Arabic); simply z in Persian

د d

ذ dh

ر r   r   Trilled as Italian initial **r**

ز z

س s   ṣ   In Arabic: a slurred s with sides of tongue curved up against palate;

ش sh

ص ṣ   in Persian: normal s

ض ḍh

ط ṭ   ḍh   In Arabic: sides of tongue curved up as with preceding letter but with tip touching back of fronth teeth;

ظ ẓ

ع '

Arabic Alphabet	Latin Alphabetic Equivalents
غ	gh
ف	f
ق	q
ک	k
ل	l
م	m
ن	n
و	w
ه	h
ی	y
ة	h,t,a*

Added Persian Consonants

پ	p
چ	ch
ژ	zh (as z in 'siezure')
گ	g (hard as in 'got')

Vowels

Long

آ	â
اُو	u
اِی	i

Short

اَ	a
اُ	o
اِ	e

Diphthongs

اَو	au
اَی	ai

	in Persian:	normal z
ṭ	In Arabic:	middle of tongue touching tip of front teeth;
	in Persian:	normal t
ẓ	In Arabic:	sides of tongue curved up and touching teeth on either side of front teeth;
	in Persian:	normal z
‘	In Arabic:	sound made by tightening of throat;
	in Persian:	glottal stop, like first letter of alphabet above
gh	In Arabic:	rolled guttural, as French r;
	in Persian	a guttural stop, similar to Arabic but not rolled
q	In Arabic:	• like a swallowed k — unvoiced;
	in Persian:	same as Persian gh — voiced

* (last letter of Arabic feminine singular nouns:

if h, noun in a final position;

if t, noun in liaison with following word;

if a, noun represented in a Persian title or text

[like Latin, Spanish or Italian feminines ending in -a used in English, which, like Persian, does not feature grammatical gender])

14

Note: 1) Arabic first names of Moslems (of Persian or whatever origin) are represented in fully elided forms to facilitate pronunciation for the English-speaking reader (examples:

عبد الرحیم Abdo'r-Rahim,

فرید الدین Farido'd-Din).

(This is the only instance where Arabic nominal inflections are represented.) 2) The ل of the Arabic article ال (al-) is shown in its conjunct form with the 'solar' letters succeeding it (example:

التوحید at-tauhid);

otherwise, the transliteration represents the written form common to both Arabic and Persian rather than the variant Persian pronunciation forms (which are indicated in the pronunciation note with each letter having a variant sound).

TRANSLATORS NOTE

References cited or quoted in the text are indicated simply by the short title of the work in question preceded by the author's surname, sobriquet or titular form used for indexing purposes; for full information on a given reference, the reader may consult the bibliography at the end of the book. Poetry is not normally given a page reference, since manuscripts and published editions vary so considerably. The exceptions are certain references to long poems of a didactic nature, segments of which appear in prose sections of this book.

Look, look — O Muslim — at the Christian
And free your mind of bias,
This rash and vain vehemence
*   — What is your real pre-eminence?*
You pretend to be the true believer
Following Mohammad; the Christian 'an infidel'
You call for following Jesus,
Despite the fact
Both are Prophets, both friends of each other.
*   Why, why — this stupid hatred of Christians?*
*   Nâṣer Khosrau (1004-1078)*

THE FATHER OF JESUS

Indubitably no man is born fatherless;
Only one Jesus exists in the world.
  — *Shabestari*

The Sufis believe that Jesus was born of Mary through the breath of the Holy Spirit, and had no physical father.

The Qoran describes the Divine animation of man as a breathing of God's Spirit into the human frame[1], using the same expression for the generation of Jesus as for the creation of Adam, that is, by a blowing of the Divine Breath, respectively, into the womb of Mary and into the clay of Adam's body — a breath which is none other than the Grace of the Holy Spirit.

Rumi[2] recounts the appearance of the Holy Spirit to Mary in the following manner:

Suspended in sheer nothing, heart-ravishing
in the Void, Mary saw a soul-stirring
Form, an enlivening Presence;

Out of the earth rose the phantom,
a Holy Spirit of Trust,
brilliant as a sun or moon;

Rapturous as the sun's aurora,

---

1. "And I breathed My Spirit into Him." *(Ḥejr,* 29 and *Ṣâd,* 72)
2. Maulânâ Jalâlo'd-Din Rumi (d. 672/1273): A great Sufi master, as well as endowed poet, he wrote the *Mathnawi* to instruct, and the *Diwân-e Shams* to inspire devotees on the Path. *(Mathnawi,* III: 3768-3785)

an apparition of naked beauty, bare and unveiled,
rose forth from the earth.

Frightened in her nakedness before the weird
Form, Mary shied back, shaking
in horror of perversion and evil.

Joseph, too, like his Egyptian lady-admirers[1]
would have cut his fingers in wonder
before the candor of such sheer beauty.

As a pure idea bursts from the heart
or the blossoming of some earthborn rose,
this imaginal form bloomed before her.

Overwhelmed by the Vision, of self bereft,
Mary swooned, entreating refuge
in the Divine Mercy;

Since her pure-bosomed nature was accustomed
to taking refuge with the Unseen
in flight from the world,

An inconstant kingdom the world appeared
to her, so prudence beckoned to make
God's patronage her fortress,

And so forge a stronghold for her soul
until death, lest any foe
waylay her quest.

Rumi's description of Mary's encounter with the

---

1. Qoran *(Yusof [Joseph]*, 31): "And when Zolaikha heard of their slanderous chatter, she sent for them and prepared cushions for them [to recline against, as guests] and gave each one a knife [and an orange to peel] and told Joseph to come out to them. Then, when they saw him, they were overwhelmed, so that they cut their hands [instead of the fruit], exclaiming, "God forgive us! This is no human being! Indeed, this can only be some beneficent angel!"

apparition[1] continues after a few lines of commentary, picking up the thread under a new chapter heading, which reads:

The Holy Spirit's declaration to Mary:
"I am an Angel from the Truth. Don't be afraid,
Nor seek to hide yourself from me."

Light sprang from his lips as he spoke,
flared up from the earth to Arcturus.
Mary, suddenly flustered, recoiled,

Distraught as a fish on the shore.
"I am the Trustee of His Spirit;
I am Majesty's consul,"

Countered the Exemplar of Charity, "Do not shrink
in shyness from such friendly spirits;
shame before such sweet confidantes is
unseemly.

"You flee from my being into Non-being
but I nestle in Non-being's milieu;
there is my dwelling, my lodging,

"My flag hoisted in Non-being's dominion,
where I reign a king. Only here,
Lady Mary, like a stray cavalier,

"My image flutters before you.
Watch, Mary, my Form's enigma,
this tangled skein of me

"You view both as a blatant moon

---

1. A reference to the Qoran *(Maryam* [*Mary*], 17-18): "We sent Out Spirit unto her, and it appeared to her in the likeness of a well-proportioned man. She said, 'I seek refuge in God from you — (that is) if you be God-fearing.' "

and an imaginal form in the heart."
— Any idea which plants itself in your heart

Stays to haunt you, wherever you wander;
except for a vain, unsubstantial fantasy,
which disappears like the false dawn. —

"I am Divine Reality's dawntide,
the Light of the Lord,
no night lurks around my day.

"Do not entreat asylum from me, invoking,
'There is no power beyond Allâh.'
I have come hither from that domain

"Where no power beyond Allâh is found;
My nourishment, my native land,
fashioned from 'No might beyond God',

"Born of a light antecedent to language,
in eternity I was the architect of God's sanctum;
yet still you seek refuge from me,

"When I myself am refuge and deliverance?"
Ah, no scourge like ignorance exists;
beside your beloved but in love's art
incompetent;

Friends you account strangers, and joys, sorrows;
confronted by a beloved of such comeliness,
faithlessly you flee. He's as graceful as a
palm,

But to us thieves, a cross and gallows;
our beloved has musk-scented tresses,
yet to us, demented, mere fetters.

Such grace which flows

as sweetly as the Nile, seems
blood to us, who are Pharaohs.

What the Sufis understand by a reference to the concept of 'Father' with respect to Jesus, such as when the Gospel quotes Jesus as saying, "I go to the Father" (John 16:16), is that the saints[1] are the spiritual children of the Divine, so that Jesus as a saint,[2] can be regarded as just such a 'spiritual offspring'.

As Rumi puts it,

My boy,
All the saints are sons of God:
Whether here or there, present or absent,
Always aware, vigilant and awake.

Shaikh Shabestari[3] provides a lyrical rendering of this concept in his *Golshan-e râz:*

First the suckling infant,
Bound to a cradle[4], is sustained on milk,[5]
Then, when mature, becomes a wayfarer;
If a man, he travels with his father.

The elements of nature for you
Resemble an earthborn mother,

---

1. Literally, in the terminology of the Qoran, the 'friends of God'.
2. In Islam all true Prophets are, by the very nature of their Prophethood, saints as well.
3. Shabestari, Shaikh Maḥmud, *Golshan-e râz (The Rosegarden of Mystery), ed.,* J.Nurbakhshsh (Tehran, 1355 AHS/1976). Shabestari (d. 740/1340): A native of the northwest Iranian province of Azarbaijan in the neighborhood of Tabriz, this influential Sufi poet and thinker enjoyed a brilliant but brief career, dying at the age of 52 or 53. His masterpiece, the *Golshan-e râz,* which was written by way of an answer to a series of questions posed by a gnostic of Herat, Mir Ḥosaini Sâdât Herawi, is a *tour de force,* encapsulating a blend of the theosophy of Ebn 'Arabi, the sage of Andalusia, and the illuminationist *(eshrâqi)* wisdom of Sohrawardi the Martyr, in 1000 lines of the most exquisite Persian poetry.
4. Lâhiji (see footnote on following page), p.678, interprets 'cradle' to mean the body.
5. According to Lâhiji, *ibid.,* 'milk' symbolizes natural attachments.

23

You, a son whose father
Is a patriarch from on high.[1]

So Jesus proclaimed upon ascension:
"I go to my Father above."[2]
You too, O favorite of your father,
Set forth for your Father![3]

Your fellow-travelers went on; you too pass on!
If you wish to be a bird in flight,
Leave the world's carcass to vultures.[4]

In his commentary on the *Golshan-e râz*, Shaikh Lâhiji[5] explains the concepts of the Holy Spirit *(ruḥ al-qodos)* and the 'Spirit of God' *(ruḥo'llâh)*, which appear in another part of Shabestari's work, verse by verse in the following manner:

Within the inner court of holy Oneness
Lies the soul's monastery,
Perch of the Simorgh of Subsistence.

(The commentator, Lâhiji): That is to say, the inner court of sanctum of holy Oneness *(waḥdat)*[6] of the Divine Essence, which transcends and is hallowed

1. Lâhiji, *ibid.*, p. 679: "The marriage of the mother of the material world with the celestial father (the spiritual world) gives birth to the human being."
2. *Âbbâ* is the Aramaic, or Syriac, word for 'father', both in the language of Jesus himself and in the vernacular of the Nestorian and Jacobite Christians to whom Shaikh Shabestari would have been exposed.
3. Lâhiji, *ibid.*, p. 679: "That is to say, depart from the abode of human attachments and interests and abandon dwelling in your physical passions and journey forth like other wayfarers on God's Path."
4. According to Lâhiji, *ibid.*, p. 680, 'vultures' signify worldly people.
5. Lâhiji. Shaikh Shamso'd-Din Moḥammad, *Sharḥ-e golshan-e râz*, ed. Kaiwân Sami'i, Tehran, 1337 AHS/1958, pp..674-6. A native of the Iranian province of Gilan on the Caspian Sea, Lâhiji was a master in the Nurbakhshi Order. He is buried in the city of Shiraz in the south of Iran.
6. The varying degrees of Oneness in Sufi metaphysics are dealt with in the author's *Sufism: Meaning, Knowledge and Unity*, New York, 1981, Chap. III.

from all blemish of multiplicity *(katharât)*, is the soul's monastery *(dair-e jân)*, and the temple *(ma'bad)* of the Christians, that is to say, the community of the prophet Jesus. Hence, the holy monastery of Divine Unity is the house of worship for the soul, the human spirit *(ruh-e ensâni)*, the origin of which is the World of Supra-Formal Entities *('âlam-e tajarrod)*. This sanctum of Divine Oneness is the soul's temple and the roost of the Simorgh of true Subsistence *(baqâ)*[1] because the wellspring and reality of Subsistence is Divine Oneness, unblemished and consecrated from all contrariness and disparity generated through mortal annihilation *(fanâ)*.[2] By realisation of this station *(maqâm)*, Jesus was graced with life and immortality.

Since pure freedom from the bondage of custom, convention, blind imitation, and habit, which Christianity *(tarsâ'i)* exemplifies, was manifested by Jesus, the poet further comments:

From the Spirit of God sprang this attainment,
Brought forth by the Holy Spirit.

The 'attainment' here implied is that of dispassion, detachment and emancipation from the bondage of multiplicity and habit, all of which Christianity represents, and consequent at-one-ment with the spiritual level and monastery of the Divine Essence in its sacred Oneness. Such labour was manifested by Jesus (as the 'Spirit of God'). No previous prophet, however graced with the virtues of perfection, ever quite attained his degree. Hence, the dictum of the Prophet Mohammad: "Of all men I am most akin to Jesus, for no other prophet appeared between him and me."

---

1. and 2. For an explanation of the concepts of *fanâ* and *baqâ*, the reader is referred to the author's *Sufism: Fear and Hope*, etc., New York, 1982, Chap. V

The determined form *(ta'ayyon)* of Jesus pertains to the innermost dimension of the All-Comprehensive Oneness of the Divine Nature, hence, his appellation, the 'Spirit of God' *(Ruho'llâh);* for he is that Perfect Spirit which is a theophany *(mazhar)* of the All-Comprehensive Name: Allâh[1]. Only the Divine Name, Allâh, and no other can serve as the 'in-spirer' (literally, 'blower into') of Jesus, by virtue of its Gabrielic form.

Jesus in his aspect of being the 'truest devotee' *('abdo'llâh-e haqiqi)* was enabled to resurrect the dead, cure the congenitally blind and heal lepers, these feats being "brought forth by the Holy Spirit *(Ruho'l-qodos)."* Total revelation of the Divine Name, Allâh, however, is too much for most people, because of their lack of spiritual capacity; so Names of a secondary nature are revealed to them.

Yet, because the human being is in essence a theophany *(mazhar)* and an object of tutelage *(marbub)* for the All-Comprehensive Name, Allâh, the poet explains that:

> *In the God-bestowed soul before you*
> *Lies a trace of sanctity manifest.*

Simply said: just as Jesus exists as the Spirit of God, likewise, a soul and reality exists present before you, who are human. "I breathed My Spirit into him" (Qoran: *Hejr,* 29 and *Sâd,* 72) is an allusion to this. In short, the human being is a theophany of the Divine Name, Allâh. By means of the inspiration of the Holy Spirit, Gabriel (who is a formal analogue for Divine Knowledge) a trace of this reality in your God-granted soul is visible. The Rational Soul *(nafs-e nâteqa)* of man is unhampered by corporeal trappings and,

---

1. That is to say, a complete mirror of the Divine Attributes. See also the section on *Jesus's Epithet.*

26

consequently, pure and divine in nature. Contemplative understanding of such a reality, however, depends upon your native aptitude, as well as your personal effort towards such realisation, until your potential resources blossom into actuality. However, because attainment of the station of Divine Oneness is impossible without prior passage through the waystations of the lower passions and natural instincts, the poet reflects:

> *If you acquit yourself of this passion-bound*
> *Soul of humanity, step within*
> *The inner court of sacred Divinity.*

By *nafs-e nasut* ('soul of humanity') is meant the state of humanity. *Lâhut* ('Divinity'), however, alludes to the reality of Divine Oneness pervading all things... While (man's) spiritual sensitivities yearn towards higher spheres, the attachments of his human and passionate nature incline him to become fixated in the baser realm of nature. So, the poet comments: "If you acquit or free yourself of this *nafs* (passion-controlled soul) of humanity *(nâsut), ...''* This soul is a subtle and vaporous substance, which acts as a bearer of the faculties of life *(hayât),* the senses *(hess)* and volitional motion *(harakat-e erâdi).* It is this which philosophers term the animal spirit *(ruh-e haiwâni),* and it is this base human soul which impedes your unification with the realm of supra-formal entities and the monastery of the Oneness of the Divine Essence. If only you could emancipate yourself of this human soul and its passions, by means of ascetic self-denial and self-effacement, then you would unquestionably attain, like Christ, the level of the inner court of Divinity *(Lâhut),* which is the level of the Oneness of the Divine Essence, and become endowed with immortality... However, because what hampers the ascension of the human rational soul to higher worlds,

27

are its egocentric and natural qualities, the poet observes,

> *Whoever, like an angel becomes detached,*
> *Liberated from matter's trappings,*
> *Ascends to the fourth heaven,*
> *Like the Spirit of God.*

Thus, whoever can extricate himself from the impositions of nature and the qualities of his passional soul, will reach a level of spirituality and supra-formal existence akin to angels. And as they are unhindered by the confines of animality and nature, he, too, as the Spirit of God (Jesus) will rise to the fourth heaven. This particular heaven is the locus and source of the *qotb* (the Pole). Revelation of such qualities to the mystic, again, depends on his personal efforts, inner struggle, innate aptitude, and his ethical character and conduct. The human being is capable of being endowed with all these virtues.

JESUS IN HIS MOTHER'S WOMB

To illustrate the telepathic nature of communication amongst saints, Rumi retells a story from the nonscriptural tradition among Moslems, relating an encounter between Mary, the mother of Jesus, and Elizabeth (Eshâ'), the mother of John the Baptist (Yaḥyâ):

Once, while she was pregnant, the mother of John found Mary, also with child, sitting before her. She told Mary that she perceived within Mary's womb "a king", who was to be a prophet of the first rank, and that she felt the child within her own womb bowing and prostrating himself in deference to the child in Mary's, and that all this was causing her terrible trial

28

and pain. Jesus, Mary replied, was doing the same prostrations in her womb.

* * *

Fools dismiss this story as just a fable and a fallacy, saying that Mary simply went off to the country and stayed by herself until she gave birth, having nothing to do with anyone else during the time of her pregnancy. They say that not even the remotest strangers saw Mary during this period, much less kith and kin, like Elizabeth [either her maternal aunt or her sister depending on the account], let alone having such an exchange occur.

However, the wise know that saints, like Mary, who are heart-conscious, have an inner vision, whereby she was perfectly capable of seeing Elizabeth and hearing these words from her, when she appeared in truth, but veiled to the profane eye.

— Rumi, *Mathnawi,*
II, vv. 3602-13

JESUS'S UTTERANCE FROM THE CRADLE

The Sufis make repeated allusions to the matter of Jesus speaking from the cradle[1]. An example is this verse from a sonnet *(ghazal)* of 'Attâr[2]:

Every Christlike saint as sweetly
as Jesus spoke such secret
words in his infancy.

1. Qoran: *Maryam (Mary),* 30-33.
2. 'Attâr, Farido'd-Din (d. 618/1221): One of the best known and prolific of the Persian Sufi poets, he wrote the classical *Manteq at-tair (The Conference of the Birds),* as well as a series of prose biographical sketches known as the *Tadhkerat al-auliyâ' (Memorial of the Saints),* among the vast number of his works, many of which are cited in this text.

29

THE CHILDHOOD OF JESUS

The Sufis believe in the natural precocity of Jesus, as Khwâja 'Abdo'llâh Anṣâri indicates in his exegesis of the Qoran[1]:

Emâm Moḥammad Bâqer says that when Jesus was nine years old, his mother committed him to the care of a tutor who told him to say, "In the Name of God, the Merciful, the Compassionate"; to which Jesus replied, "In the Name of God." Then the preceptor told him to recite the *abjad*.[2] Jesus repeated it in this fashion: *"Alef* stands for the *âlâ* (graces) from God, *bâ'* for the *behjat* (joy) in God, *jim* for the *jalâl* (Majesty) of God, and *dâl* for the *din* (faith) of God." The preceptor told Mary to take her son by the hand and depart, for he had no need of teaching or tutelage.

THE PASSING OF JESUS

Grieve not that Mary's gone;
The light that Jesus heavenward bore,
has come.

— Rumi

1. Anṣâri, Khwâja 'Abdo'llâh, *Tafsir-e 'erfani wa adabi-ye qor'ân-e majid*, ed. Ḥabibo'llâh Âmuzegâr, Tehran, 1348 AHS/1969, vol.II, p. 30. Renowned as the Pir of Herat, Khwâja 'Abdo'llâh (d. 481/1088) was both a clerical authority in the field of Sunni jurisprudence in the Hanbali school *(madhhab)*, and a Sufi master of great importance. His exegesis is unique in that it brings together both canonical and gnostic interpretations, and is regarded as authoritative by Sufis, as well as by the exoteric clergy. In addition to this impressive ten-volume work, the master produced a collection of mystical *monâjât* (supplicatory prayers), which have served as inspiration for devotees for centuries. He was a disciple of the famous Abo'l-ḥasan Kharaqâni and an associate of another master, Abu Sa'id Abe'l-Khair.

2. *Abjad*: The name for the numerological order of the Arabic alphabet, being an acronym composed of the first four letters in the system, which follows the order of the Hebrew and Syriac alphabets. These letters in Arabic are *alef, bâ, jim* and *dâl*.

The Sufis believe that Jesus, in attaining the station of human perfection, achieved complete union with the Divine, and they understand his ascension as the passage to a more exalted realm of being.

As Shaikh Ruzbehân puts it:[1]

Look at the truth of the matter. As his body turned to spirit, his outward form became entirely soul, and he disappeared from the dust. How could accident affect him? Don't you see that when it was all over, Jesus ascended into heaven?

In another place he says:[2]

As the lover becomes exalted in love, when love returns to its motherlode, it turns the lover to its own hue, spiriting him back to the presence of the Beloved, that he may soar as the saintly ones of the angelic realm with the most splendidly plumed of the seraphim in the empyrean heights of the exalted beings,[3] even as Khedhr and Elias and Jesus — when their human qualities became Divine Attributes, their substance became ethereal.

JESUS'S EPITHET

Sufis say that the epithet of highest honor bestowed by God is 'Abdo'llah ('the slave [or devotee] of God'), where the honor comes in linking the Creator with the created in

---

1. Baqli, Shaikh Ruzbehân, *Sharh-e shathiyât*, ed., Henry Corbin, Tehran, 1360 AHS/1981, pp. 46-7.
2. Baqli, *'Abhar al-'âsheqin*, ed., J. Nurbakhsh, Tehran, 1349 AHS/1970.
3. 'The exalted beings' is a rendering of '*Elliyun*, the deliberately obscure term used in the Qoran for beings whose station is far beyond material human comprehension: "No, indeed, the record [of the deeds] of the righteous is with [in the paradise of] the 'Elliyun. Now, can you come to understand what the 'Elliyun are?" *Motaffefin (The Cheaters),* 18-19.

31

one name.

God has singled out amongst His Prophets only two individuals to be dubbed 'devotees': just Mohammad and Jesus.

Referring to Mohammad, the Qoran has an account beginning with the sentence: "And when the Devotee of God stood up..." *(Jinn, 19)*

With respect to Jesus, the Qoran has Jesus declaring (from the cradle): "I am the Devotee of God; God has granted me the Scripture..." *(Maryam [Mary], 30).*

The Sufis believe that ' 'Abdo'llâh' denotes the perfect devotee, upon whom the Almighty has manifested all His Names; that he is the epitome of all that 'devotee' signifies; and, having realized the Name of God, which is the highest name and which embraces the whole of the Divine Attributes, he reaches the serenest of stations and the sublimest degree of perfection to which humanity can attain.

THE ACQUISITION OF A GODLY CHARACTER

The Sufis look upon Jesus as manifestation of the Divine Attributes of Creator and Reviver and Mary as manifestation of the Attribute of Sustainer.

Najmo'd-Din Râzi[1] explains it in this way:

When [the Divine] is manifested in the Attribute of Sustainer, it is expressed in the form of Mary [as when she feeds herself, being with child, having retreated in solitude to give birth, upon the Divine instruction]: "And shake the trunk of the palmtree

---

1. Râzi, Najmo'd-Din (d. 1256 AD): Author of the *Merṣâd al-'ebâd*, his most famous work, which appeared in 1226 AD and rapidly became a handbook for Sufis throughout the Persian-speaking world, from Turkey to India, he was a disciple of Najmo'd-Din Kobrâ and a contemporary of Maulânâ Jalâlo'd-Din Rumi, poet, master and author of the *Mathnawi*, whom he met late in life.

toward yourself, so that the ripened dates may fall for you (and you may take them as your repast)." *(Maryam [Mary], 25).*

In the case of Jesus as manifestation of the Attribute of Creator, God reminds Jesus how "you made the likeness of a bird out of clay and breathed into it, and it became a bird with My permission..." *(Mâ'edah [The Table Spread],* 110).

And the same verse continues with an example of Jesus manifesting the Attribute of Reviver: "... and you raised the dead with My permission..."

What is meant by the perfected human being as 'manifestation' is that such a human is not the source but merely a mirror reflecting the Attributes, which emanate from the Divine possessor of those qualities.

THE SPIRITUAL STATION OF JESUS

The gnostics amongst the Sufis distinguish four kinds of sainthood *(welâyat):*[1]

1. That which is the inner dimension of prophethood *(nabowwat)* as such.

2. That which is confined to *(moqayyedah)* a given prophet.

3. That which is absolute *(moṭlaqah)* within every prophet.

4. That which is common *('âmmah)* (that is, attainable by all who seek it).[2]

---

1. Welâyat literally means 'friendship' with God, referring to the relationship between the saints *(auliyâ':* literally, 'friends') and God, as in the Qoranic verse which refers to them as those "whom He loves and who love Him" *(Mâ'edah [The Table Spread],* 54). In loving Him, they are drawn to Him, and, through this attraction, turn from their attachment to the fleshly world; progressing to the point where God may confer sainthood upon them.

2. The goal of common sainthood is for the devotee, in reaching the ultimate station of traveling towards God, to become annihilated in the Essence and Attributes of the Divine, while retaining the potential for separate existence with respect to himself. (Author's note)

The Sufis say that common sainthood began with Adam and ended with Jesus, who is the Seal of Common Sainthood.

THE WAY OF JESUS AND HIS METHOD

The way of Jesus was the path of striving, of seclusion and of self-abnegation. In a Sufi manner, he enjoyed solitude and disliked ceremony, being detached from the world and its attractions.

Hasan Baṣri[1] said of Jesus that he "dressed in coarse wool, ate what he could pluck from trees, and slept wherever night found him."[2]

Jesus was the ascetic amongst the prophets, attaining the highest station of asceticism, which is total abandonment of the world.

Jesus was dedicated to poverty *(faqr)*[3], and his practice of poverty is proverbial.

'Aṭṭâr gives an account of this in his *Tadhkerat al-auliyâ'*.[4]

Jonaid[5] said: "The Sufi is one whose heart, like Abraham's, has become immune from attachment to

---

1. Hasan Basri (d. 110/728): The famous master of the first generation of Sufis after the age of Moḥammad, he was the disciple of 'Ali.
2. Anonymous, *Kholâṣa-ye sharḥ-e ta'arrof,* ed., Aḥmad 'Ali Rajâ'i, Tehran, 1349 AHS/1970, p. 40. One of the earliest works on Sufism in Persian, this book is a summary of the commentary made by Abu Ebrâhim Bokhârâ'i (d. 434/1042-43) on the Arabic-language *Ta'arrof li-madhhab ahl at-taṣawwof* by Abu Bakr Moḥammad Kalâbâdhi (d. 990 or 994), which has been partially translated into English by A.J. Arberry as *The Doctrine of the Sufis* (Cambridge, 1977). The full Persian text of the commentary was published in four vols. in Lucknow, 1330/1912.
3. *Faqr:* (literally, 'poverty', that is to say, 'poverty in spirit') having nothing but God. Our forthcoming book on *faqr* is entirely devoted to this subject.
4. This account is found also in Hojwiri's *Kashf al-maḥjub.*
5. Shaikh Abo'l-Qâsem Jonaid Baghdâdi (d. 298/910): The celebrated master whose leadership of the 'Baghdad School' of Sufism in his day did a great deal to win acceptance for the mystical path amongst the legalist divines.

the world and complies with God's command; and whose submission is that of Ishmael, and whose sorrow is that of David, and whose poverty is that of Jesus, and whose patience is that of Job, and whose yearning is that of Moses engaged in prayer of supplication, and whose sincerity is that of Moḥammad."

A
GLOSSARY
OF
SUFI TERMS
RELATING
TO
CHRISTIANITY

JESUS[1]

In Sufi terminology, the name of Jesus stands for 'Love', while the 'Jesus-' or 'Christ-breath' represents the Perfect Master.

> *Know possessions as the Antichrist,*
> *and look on Jesus as love.*
> *Once you've joined the band of Jesus,*
> *you can slit the other's throat.*

— Sanâ'i

> *Happy news, O heart!*
> *The Jesus-breath has come!*
> *From his wholesome spirit*
> *wafts the fragrance of the One.*

— Hâfez

CHRISTIAN *(tarsâ)*

[This word means, literally, 'God-fearing', 'pious'.]

This term as used by the Sufis symbolically, in poetry has various connotations:

1) Someone who has yet to be liberated from ego-consciousness.

In the words of Hâfez:[2]

---

1. After this entry, the terms are given in alphabetical order.
2. Shamso'd-Din Mohammad Hâfez (d. 792/1389): The sonnet-like poems *(ghazal-s)* of this greatest of poets of the Path, master-pieces of the Persian poetic art, are amongst the highest reflections of the states of the Sufi Path ever put on paper. The classic edition of Hâfez's Diwân is that of Mohammad Qazwini, which is regularly reprinted in Tehran. The most scholarly is the edition of Mas'ud Farzâd, cited in the bibliography at the back of the book.

How sweet it was to hear a Christian chant
This verse to his flute and daf
One morningtide beside
The tavern doorway:

> *— If this is Islam,*
> *which Ḥâfez upholds,*
> *woe the morrow*
> *which follows upon today!*

2) A perfect master and perfecting master who is the focus of attraction for all things, whether naturally or volitionally.

3) A spiritually devoted person who is in the process of transforming the undesirable traits of his 'demanding ego' *(nafs-e ammâra)* into meritorious ones.

— *Kashshâf estelâhât-al fonun*

4) A *mowwahed* (that is to say, someone who is immersed in the Divine Unity *(tauhid).*

— *Kashshâf estelâhât-al fonun*

CHRISTIANITY *(tarsâ'i)*

1) The state of detachment (from both the world and the hereafter and from any desire for compensation) *(tajrid)* and self-abnegation (involving singleness and solitude in devotion) *(tafrid).*

In the context of Shaikh Shabestari:
> *Non-attachment and detachment —*
> *Freedom from the fetters of imitation —*
> *Are the pith and whole design*
> *I see in Christianity.*

40

2) As defined by 'Erâqi[1] in his dictionary of terms:

"The inner meanings and truths (of things)
when realized in their precise and subtle forms."
— *Estelâhât-e 'erâqi*

3) As defined by Darwish Mohammad Tabasi[2]:

"The theophany of Beauty and the perception of
truths and essences."
— *Äthâr-e tabasi*

CHRISTIAN CHILD *(tarsâ-bachcha or tarsâ-zâda)*

1) Variously, an aspirant on the Path or a perfect
master whose soul has become purified of undesirable traits,
called so because the persuasion of such an individual is
actually trinitarian, embracing the tripartite aspects of God,
himself and his search.

As Shaikh Shabestari expresses it:

Give up your heart to the Christian child;
Free yourself of all denial and affirmation.

In 'Attâr's words:

The Christian child again stalks my soul
and haunts my heart, her tresses have
infatuated me, disgraced me

1. Fakhro'd-Din 'Erâqi (d. 688/1289): One of the greatest Sufi poets, he had
several masters, including Sadro'd-Din Qonyawi, who provided the key systematic
formulation of the philosophy of Ebn 'Arabi. His poetry is amongst the highest
achievements of purely ecstatic expression, expounding the vision of the Beloved
through contemplation of theophanies, or Divine manifestations, in the context of
a medium which presents a lyrical sublimation of the philosophy of *wahdat al-
wojud* (the 'Unity of Being'). The reader is referred to 'Iraqi, Fakhruddin, *Divine
Flashes,* trans., W.C. Chittick and P.L. Wilson, London, 1982.
2. Darwish Mohammad Tabasi: A shaikh of Shâh Ne'mato'llâh Vali (d.
834/1437), the founder of the Ne'mato'llâhi Order.

41

Before the world, while my heart
I've given up; I've gone wrong;
    my one pain made a thousandfold...
But what I've done,
    I've done myself,
    what can I do with myself?

And in the verse of Ḥâfeẓ:

Last night the Christian child commented —
What a shame, Ḥâfeẓ, what a waste,
To watch you clamoring
At a different temple every moment.

2) The Christian child, furthermore, symbolizes influxes from the spiritual world.

3) In Sufi terminology, the Christian child may also represent one who, as the result of a state of theophany, witnesses a Divine manifestation.

CHURCH *(kelisâ)*

1) In the Sufi vocabulary, the 'church' stands for the realm of confusion and consternation *(hairat)*.
— Tabasi, *op.cit.*

2) It is also a reference to the realm of certainty *(yaqin)*.

3) It may represent the state of manifestation *(zohur)*.

CHURCHBELL *(nâqus)*

1) Recollection of the station of distractedness with the world *(tafraqa)*
— 'Erâqi, *op. cit.*

2) Reference to the abandonment of any claim to name and fame.

3) Furthermore, an allusion to the awakening which leads to penitence and the undertaking of devotion.
— *Kashshâf estelâhât-al fonun*

4) Also, the attraction that comes from the Divine and

clears the soul, drawing it to devotion and contented abstinence *(qanâ'at),* stirring it from the sleep of forgetfulness *(gheflat).*

— Kashshäf estelähät-al fonun

CLOISTER *seume'a (also 'hermitage')*

1). It may be used in its literal sense as Hafez employs it:

Reverend puritan —
  past is the time
    you might see me
      frequenting the cloister abbey;

I've taken a different
  chargé d'affaires:
    the Saqi's visage,
      the Cup's lip.

Were the standards of the hermitage
  once assayed in reality,
The hermits would all desert their cells
  and start job-hunting.

2. In Sufi terms, it symbolizes an assembly of gnostics and saints.

— Hedâyat, Riyâdh al-'ârefin,

CROSS *(chalipâ or salib)*

1) The realm of natures, tempers, dispositions *(tabâye').*

— Tabasi, op. cit.

As Rumi applies it:

Who stirs, who rustles,
  her ringlet's linked locks?
Whose faith is preserved

43

from the crucifix of her curls?

2) Also refers to the Attribute of the Divine Majesty
(jalâl).

CINCTURE *(zonnâr)*

In its conventional meanings, it may signify:
1) The cord from which the cross carried by a
Christian is hung.
2) The cord which Zoroastrians wear tied around the
waist.
3) The cord which Christians, as an officially protected
minority in Islamically-ruled domains, were formerly
required to wear to distinguish themselves from the Moslem
majority.
As Rumi uses the term:

I've bound a cincture of blasphemy
beneath this holy gown of piety,
Which proclaims out loud my infamy
in every town.

And in the words of Ṣâ'eb of Tabriz:

My religion is uprooted,
my faith's a shambles;
call me Theewards —
Quick! so I'll unbind
this cincture of dualism
from my waist.

Its Sufi meanings include:
1) The sign of perfect adherence to the way of certainty
and commitment to the master.
2) Reference to the belt of service, girded with a vow of
resolution to follow the Divine.
In the verse of Shaikh Shabestari:

When I contemplated the active principle of every
matter,
I saw the cincture's knot implied,
A bond of service tied,
For only in the context of their primary conditions
Can things by sages be acknowledged.
Like real men, enter the company of the Covenant,[1]
Loins girded for work;
On the steed of knowledge,
Wield devotion's stave;
Carry fortune's ball from the field.
The purpose of your creation
In such labor lies.
Despite the numberless other beings generated,
Knowledge is your father;
Mother, the deed done,
Their offspring, your state in between.

As Ḥâfeẓ applies the term in one place:

Piety I might sell; abstinence I'd hawk;
Even gird myself again with a cincture,
laboring in your quarter,
But never will I sell my dervish cassock.

And in another:

The Sufi habit I owned, well —
served to hide my faults
(over a hundred)...
Then I pawned my cassock for wine
and hired some minstrels;
now only a cincture remains.

---

1. Qoran: *Baqarah (The Cow)*, 40: "O Children of Israel! Remember My favor which I have bestowed upon you, and honor the Covenant which you have made with Me, that I may honor Mine with you, and fear Me."

45

3. Furthermore, in Sufi terms, the 'cincture' indicates the seeking to grasp the 'firm rope' *(ḥabl-e matin)*, which is the Beloved.

MONASTERY *(dair)*

In Sufi terminology, the 'monastery' means the realm of inner significance and of the highest refinement of humanity, as well as the inner being of the perfect gnostic.
In the verse of Narâqi:

> *In the end, we left the Ka'ba,*
> *moved to the monastery;*
> *Thank God for such sheer fortune,*
> *for such a blessed sequel — God be praised!*

And as Jâmi uses the term:

> *Go, dwell in a monastery, among those whom Jesus inspires;*
> *Move your home out of the way of strangers.*

MONK (râheb)

One who flees from falsehood *(baṭel)* to the truth *(ḥaqq)* or from multiplicity, *(kathrat)* to Unity *(waḥdat)*.
— Mer'ât 'oshâq[1]
In the verse of Shaikh Shabestari:

---

1. Reference is page 199 in the Bertels study of Sufism: cf. bibliography under Bertels Y.E.

Adopt the primordial faith[1]
Free of all shackles, of all sects;
Step into real religion's
Monastery as a monk.

TRINITY *(tathlith)*

While the conventional Christian doctrine of the Trinity is expressed in the concepts of Father, Son and Holy Spirit, Hâtef of Esfahan provides a Sufi interpretation in his famous *tarji'-band* (a balladic form of stanzas with interposed refrain):

"Lured by you, my heart is entangled
    in your snare," I pleaded in church
To a Christian maiden,
    "as though every stray strand of my hair
Were enmeshed in your cincture's skeins.
    How long will Unity's way remain unfound? Till
when will the One stand defamed by the trinity?
    How can it be laudable to call God The
Absolute, the Single, with Names like
    Father, Son and Holy Ghost?"
She parted her sugar-drenched lips,
    which disparaged sugar itself, and said:
"Were only you conscious of Unity's mystery,
    you'd never name me 'infidel'.
The radiant visage of Eternal Beauty

---

1. The word used here by Shaikh Shabestari is *hanifi*. According to the *Shorter Encyclopedia of Islam* (ed., H.A.R. Gibb and J.H. Kramers, Leiden, 1974, p. 132), this word "appears repeatedly in the Qoran as the name of those who possess the real and true religion; e.g. in Sura X, 105; XXII, 31; XXX, 30; XCVIII, 4, etc. It is used particularly of Abraham as the representative of the pure worship of God. As a rule it contrasts him with the idolaters as in III, 95; VI, 79, 161; X, 105; XVI, 120, 123; XXII, 31, but in one or two passages describes him as one who was neither a Jew nor a Christian... Sura XXX, 30, is of special importance for understanding the Qoranic meaning of the word, where it is said: "Turn thy face [i.e, purpose] towards the primordial religion of the upright *(hanif)* — the nature innately formed by God, in which He hath created man."

illuminated three distinct mirrors;
Silk is not threefold in kind
      if named parniyân, harir *or* parand"[1]
Engaged in this parley, suddenly
I heard the churchbells chime:

      There is only one;
        nothing exists but He;
          He is one;
             no god but He exists.

---

1. Three Persian words all meaning 'silk'.

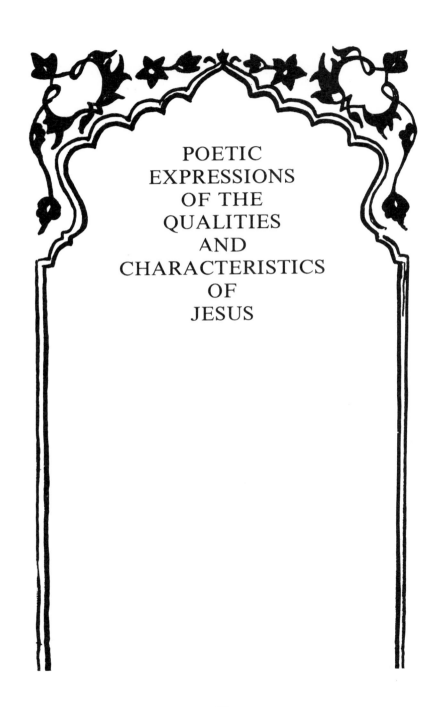

POETIC EXPRESSIONS OF THE QUALITIES AND CHARACTERISTICS OF JESUS

THE BREATH OF JESUS

Given the fact that by his breath Jesus brought the dead
to life and healed the sick, Sufi poets have been inspired to
draw allusions and metaphors out of the phenomenon of the
breath of Jesus.

When God shadowed grace on the breath of Jesus,
The world was filled with passion.
— 'Attâr, Mosibat-nâma

The dawn, remembering you, laughed,
*   bringing all beings to life*
*   with that Jesus-like breath.*
— 'Attâr, Mosibat-nâma

The east wind bearing the fragrance of your tresses,
*   gives life to the breath of Jesus.*
Contemplation of your countenance
*   illumines the eyes of Moses.*
— 'Attâr, Diwân

This breath of Jesus, which hourly brings forth
Another dawn, causes a sleeping world
To raise its head from the earth.
— 'Attâr, Diwân

As 'Attar's words give life to the soul,
Clearly he is of the same breath as Jesus.
— 'Attâr, Diwân

The breath of Jesus is merely a subtlety
*   of your ruby lips;*

51

The water of life is only a hint
of the sweetness of your mouth.

— Hâfez, *Diwân*

Remember that when your eye's reproach slew me,
On your sugary lips lay the reviving breath of Jesus.

— Hâfez, *Diwân*

Love's physician is compassionate and endowed
With the breath of Jesus,
But whom should he assuage,
If you are without pain?

— Hâfez, *Diwân*

The breath of Christ
That brought the dead to life
Was but one breath
Of My Divine Breath,
The nurturer of Spirits.

— 'Erâqi, *Resâla-ye Lama'ât*[1]

With one breath you revive a hundred dead souls.
Who are you?
Christ, a spirit, or the Water of Life?

— 'Erâqi, *Diwân*

To whom may I relate such a subtlety?
She killed me — my stony-hearted mistress,
Yet possessed that life-giving breath of Jesus.

— Hâfez, *Diwân*

Grief's burden wearied us
Until God sent someone whose breath, like Jesus
Could lighten and uplift that weight.

— Hâfez, *Diwân*

O You! Who sometimes revive this earthen flesh

1. P. 2.

52

Like Jesus, with a breath,
And sometimes show up beneath the gallows
Like Ḥạllaj... Come!
— Rumi, *Diwân-e shams*

THE SINCERITY OF JESUS

One should be as Jesus, son of Mary,
On the way of sincerity,
To grasp the value and verity of the chapter
And verse of the Gospel.
— Sanâ'i, *Diwân,*

THE CERTAINTY OF JESUS

If you claim to be a prophet like Jesus,
You will not be accepted,
Unless you make your certainty that of Jesus,
Then, call yourself the Messiah.
— Sanâ'i, *Diwân,*

THE DETACHMENT OF JESUS

Gold and women are nothing but instigators of sorrow;
Leave them behind, like Jesus, son of Mary.
— Shabestari, *Golshan-e râz*

If for only a moment you free yourself
From this prison around you,
You will be like Jesus,
Unique in detachment.
— 'Aṭṭâr, *Diwân*

THE PURITY OF JESUS

Cleanse me, O Lord, of this filthy soul,

So I may claim immortal purity for myself, like Jesus.
— 'Attâr, *Diwân*

JESUS THE LOGOS (WORD OF GOD)

Were he not the Word of God,
How should Jesus be honored
*   as 'Absolute Spirit'?*
— Attâr, *Elâhi-nâma*

THE SECLUSION OF JESUS

Jesus sought, by seclusion,
To set the world aside;
Till his Beloved conceded him closeness
To his heart's desires.
— Sa'di, *Qasâ'ed*

JESUS'S WALKING ON WATER

Water became firm earth under the soles of Jesus;
The moribund earth was quickened by his pure breath.
— 'Attâr, *Mosibat-nâma*

Then, like Jesus,
You'll walk on water,
Accompany the sun,
Pace by the moon!
— Sanâ'i, *Hadiqat al-haqiqah*

JESUS'S NEEDLE

Beloved! Your mouth is as tiny as the eye
Of the needle of Jesus, and your waist as slim
As the thread of Mary's spindle.
— 'Attâr, *Diwân*

Jesus flew to heaven
On the pinions of wisdom.
 Had his donkey half a wing
To fly with, he'd escape asininity.

— Sanâ'i, *Diwân*

When you may intimately confide in Jesus,
Why be yoked in friendship with an ass?
When you can live in holy seclusion with Christ,
Why be in league with a donkey's lust?

— 'Aṭṭâr, *Elâhi-nâma*

Like an ass in a daze you lie,
Steeped in your animal passions,
Nigh unto the inferno.
So, make haste to rise into heaven, like Jesus!

— 'Aṭṭâr, *Diwân*

The Jesus of your heart is all
But dead of emaciation,
While you're still in bondage
To feeding this asinine flesh.

— Sa'di, *Qasâ'ed*

Into the farthest firmament
 souls mount, borne aloft.
Why worry if the way is barred
 to an ass's cadaver?

— Rumi, *Diwân-e shams*

You may take the ass of Jesus to Mecca,
But come home again —
 it's still an ass.

— Sa'di, *Golestân*[1]

1. Chap. VII.

55

'The ass of Jesus' is defined in the dictionary of the late scholar Sa'id Nafisi as 'an ascetic living in seclusion'.

METAPHORICAL TITLES FOR JESUS

THE 'JESUS OF THE SOUL'

You are both my heart's lark
And the Jesus of my soul;
If anyone like You exists,
That, too, is You.

— Nezâmi, *Makhzan al-asrâr*

Those still enthralled by this prison of the flesh
Cannot distinguish the soul's Jesus
From this corporeal frame.

— Shâh Qâsem Anwâr, *Diwân*

Only when the 'Jesus of the Soul'
Turns away from the world
May one soar in spiritual flight
Beyond the azure vault of the skies.

— Rumi, *Diwân-e shams*

THE 'JESUS OF THE AGE'

You are the Jesus of your age,
Assuaging those deadened by greed
And healing the heedless
*   by your spiritual breath.*

— Sanâ'i, *Diwân*

THE 'JESUS OF THE ZEPHYR'

May your every moment be merry!

O Jesus of the Zephyr!
As you've revived Hâfez's heartworn spirit
by a breath.

— Hâfez, *Diwân*

THE 'JESUS OF THE BREATH'

My soul was swept away by a heady wine;
Hâfez by love consumed —
Ah, where's someone inspired with
Jesus's breath to revive me?

— Hâfez, *Diwân*

THE 'JESUS OF LOVE'

When Jesus, Love's spirit, takes flight,
Never again will he lower his wing
To return to the realm of labor.

— Rumi, *Diwân-e shams*

THE 'JESUS OF THE SPIRIT'

Leave argumentation to the Antichrist
and befriend the 'Jesus of the Spirit'

— 'Attâr, *Diwân*

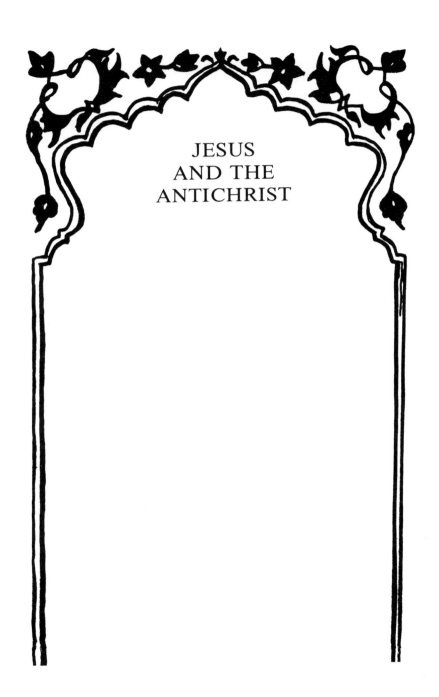

JESUS
AND THE
ANTICHRIST

The Islamic word for 'Antichrist', *Dajjâl,* literally means 'the ultimate liar',[1] it refers to the pseudo-Messiah who appears with the rightful one (Jesus) at the end of time, claiming divinity for himself.

The Sufis distinguish the true Jesus as 'spirit' and the Antichrist as the 'demanding ego' *(nafs-e ammâra)* in their symbolic terminology. Najmo'd-Din Râzi[2] compares the two in the following manner:

Now, in exposition of the truth about Jesus and the Antichrist and the respective similarity and contrast between them, it may be said that the similarity is superficial and the contrast fundamental. From the point of view of appearance, they are both called the 'Messiah', and both have a donkey, and they are both alive, and they both bring the dead to life.

Now, Jesus is called the 'Messiah' through traveling the heavens, while the Antichrist is called the 'Messiah' by traveling through the earth from east to west. Jesus is heavenly and the Antichrist is earthly.

---

1. The apocalyptic appearance of the Antichrist figures in the eschatological tales of the Moslem tradition in the same spirit as it does in the Christian in the description of the Second Coming at the end of time. The name for the Antichrist in Arabic is Dajjâl, connected with the Syriac 'daggâl', with a Semitic root meaning 'to deceive'. The reader is referred to the *Shorter Encyclopedia of Islam,* compiled by H.A.R. Gibb and J.B. Kramers, Leiden, 1974, p.67, for a discussion on the subject.
2. Râzi, Najmo'd-Din, *Marmuzât-e asadi dar mazmurât-e dâ'udi,* ed., Mohammad Redha Shafi'i Kadkani, Tehran, 1352 AHS/1973. Author also of the more famous *Mersâd al-'ebâd.* Râzi (d. 654/1256) has provided some of the most cogent descriptions of Sufi psychology and the method of the spiritual Path. He was a disciple of the 'master of masters' Najmo'd-Din Kobrâ and was a contemporary of Rumi.

Jesus has vision and confers vision on others; visionary because in his infancy he said, "Indeed, I am the devotee of God,"[1] and conferring vision by virtue of healing "the blind and the leper,"[2] while the Antichrist is blind and a blinder of others, for he presents the Truth as falsehood and falsehood as the Truth. Now, Jesus brings the dead to life as a miracle to provide grounds for faith, while the Antichrist quickens the dead as a demonstration of powers to lure one into denying faith. And the emergence of the Antichrist out of the earth serves to bring about a reign of oppression and corruption on earth, while the descent of Jesus from heaven is to bring about a reign of equity and justice.

Be aware that all is in the realm of form is a reflection of that which is in the realm of spirit, and all that is in the realms of form and spirit is represented in man.

Hence, the 'Jesus-ness' in you is your spirit, as of Jesus it is said: "We breathed of Our Spirit into it [Mary's womb]" *(Taḥrim [The Banning]*, 12), while of you it is said: "I breathed of My Spirit into him [Adam]" *(Ḥejr,* 29)[3]. Jesus brings the dead to life, as the spirit brings life to the lifeless frame. Jesus had a mother, whereas the Divine Breath served in place of a father for him; likewise, the spirit (of each person) is mothered by the elements and fathered by the Breath. Jesus is sublime, and the spirit is sublime; Jesus is the Word, and the spirit is the Word, as indicated by the expression that the "spirit is by command of my Lord" *(Esrâ' [The Night Ascension]*, 85). Jesus rode a donkey, as the spirit rides the body.

And the Antichrist is represented in you as your

---

1. *Maryam (Mary), 30*
2. *Âle 'emrân (The Family of Imran),* 49; also *Mâ'edah (The Table Spread),* 110
3. Also, *Ṣâd,* 72

'demanding ego'. The Antichrist is one-eyed, just like your ego, seeing only the world and being blind to the hereafter. Whatever the Antichrist presents as heaven is actually hell, and what he presents as hell is really heaven; by the same token, the ego presents carnal passions and pleasures as paradisical, though they are actually infernal, and it presents one's spiritual devotion and worship as hellish, though they are really heavenly in nature.

The Antichrist mounts a donkey, and your ego possesses bestial qualities. The mystery of it all is that, though Jesus was in the world, as was the Antichrist, Jesus was carried up to heaven for a while, while the Antichrist was locked up in the bowels of the earth. Then, the Antichrist will first be brought out to rampage over the earth and create havoc and wreak corruption, claiming divinity. Next, Jesus will be brought down and given dominion, claiming to be the devotee of God. He will succeed in slaying the Antichrist, then set about establishing a reign of prosperity, justice and equity. After a time, he will pass from this world, and the Day of Judgment will be at hand.

In the same way, spirit and ego are brought together in the world of humanity. However, the spirit is taken up to the heaven of the heart, while the Antichrist of the ego is confined in the earth of the human state. It takes several years for humanity to develop its full potential and for the constituents of the body to properly mature. First, the Antichrist of the ego emerges from the confines of infancy, mounted on the ass of animal qualities, launching forth on its program of wreaking havoc in the world, claiming divinity in the manner of "Have you seen the one who makes his desire his god...?" *(Jâthiyah [Kneeling], 23),* and exhorting one towards the hell of greed and lust as the heavenly goal, while decrying the heaven of devotion and worship as hell. He slays the believers of praiseworthy, angelic qualities with the unbelievers' hands of satanic and condemnable qualities, raising the dead powers in human nature, until, all of a sudden, a grace unimaginable bears from on high the Jesus of spirituality, mounted on the regal wings of the Gabriel of the Law, taking flight from the lofty heaven of the heart to descend into the world of humanity.

Reason, left behind, gazes at his departing stirrup,
While Love surges ahead, mounted by his side.

Jesus slays the Antichrist of the ego, by severing his head of material nature, and establishes the dominion of the justice and equity of spirituality in the world of humanity, destroying the swine of greed, shattering the cross of fleshly nature, and slashing the bonds of passion.

— Râzi, *Marmuzât-e asadi,*
pp.140-142

GOD'S
WORDS
TO
JESUS

1. "It was revealed to Jesus: 'O Jesus, you will not attain what you desire, until you have patiently put up with what you do not care for.' "   — Anṣâri, *Tafsir-e 'erfâni,* p. 520

2) "God revealed to Jesus: 'Keep yourself hungry, that you may see Me; and be detached, that you may be joined to Me.' " — Râzi, *Mersâd al-'ebâd,* p.330.

In this context, it might be appropriate to quote an apt quatrain from an anonymous poet on the subject of detachment:

Twig and leaf sprout from earth-planted root;
  The seed humbly buried sends up a shoot.
Goalward-bound is the one detached;
  No plumes appear on a chick unhatched.

3) "God revealed to Jesus, Son of Mary: 'Whenever you seek to advise people, counsel your own self first; once you have done that, then give advice to others; otherwise, take shame before Me.' " — Solami, *'Oyub an-nafs,* cited in Qoshairi, p.457.

4) "God revealed to Jesus: 'When I bestow upon you a blessing, receive it with humble gratitude, that I may lavish upon you My entire Bounty.' " — Ghazâli, Abu Hâmed, *Ehyâ' al-'olum,* vol. IV, p.945.

5) "God revealed to Jesus: 'When I come to find that the heart of a devotee is free of love for the world and the

hereafter, I fill it with My Love.' " — Qoshairi, *op. cit.,* p.620.

6) "They say that Jesus once declared, 'Every termite has its nest, while I haven't even a ruin.' A thundering came from the Lord: 'I am the refuge of the wanderers and the hearth of the homeless.' " — Anṣâri, *op. cit.,* p.436.

7) "The Divine addressed Jesus, saying, 'If you seek to soar in heaven with the angels, be like the owl. Amongst the birds, the owl is one which is especially prudent. And in humanity, be like the earth under the feet of people; and in generosity, be like flowing water with people. And in loving-kindness, be like the sun, which shines with equal favor on all alike.' " — Abu Bakr Moḥammad ebn 'Abdo'l-Karim, *Ferdaus al-morshediyah,* p.200.

8) "In the Gospel[1] it is stated that God said to Jesus: 'Remember Me when you are angry and I shall remember you when I am angered. And be content with My succor, for My help towards you is better for you than your own attempts to aid yourself.' " — Qoshairi, *op. cit.,* p.470.

9) "In the Gospel it is stated: 'O son of man, if I bestow wealth and power on you, you become involved in it, and if I make you poor, you become despondent and regretful. So how can you ever discover the sweetness of remembrance of Me? When will you hasten to go about worshipping Me?' " — Sa'di, *Golestân.*

10) "In the Gospel it is stated: 'O son of man, I do not expect any justice of you in your actions day by day while you expect your measure of sustenance from me each day.' " — Kâshâni, *Meṣbâḥ al-hedâyah,* p.399.

11) "In the accounts it has been recorded: 'Verily, I say

---

1. References to the Gospel in Sufi writings seem to stem from what Christian orthodoxy would call the 'apocryphal' tradition.

unto you that if your eyes were to view what I have in store for My righteous devotees, you would stop obeying your ego.' " — Hamadhâni, *Nâmahâ*, p.433.

JESUS'S PRAYER

Ghazali[1] tells us that, according to tradition, Jesus used to say the following prayer:

O Lord, verily have I arrived at the state where I am incapable of repelling that which I do not care for or of acquiring that which I aspire to have, and where the control of matters is out of my hands, and where I am subject to my actions; and there is no pauper more impoverished than I.

O Lord, let not my enemies rejoice, nor turn my friends against me, nor visit affliction on me with respect to my faith, nor make the world my greatest concern, nor let those who are ruthless towards me have power over me.

---

1. Ghazâli, Abu Hâmed, *Ehyâ' al-'olum*, vol. II, p. 455

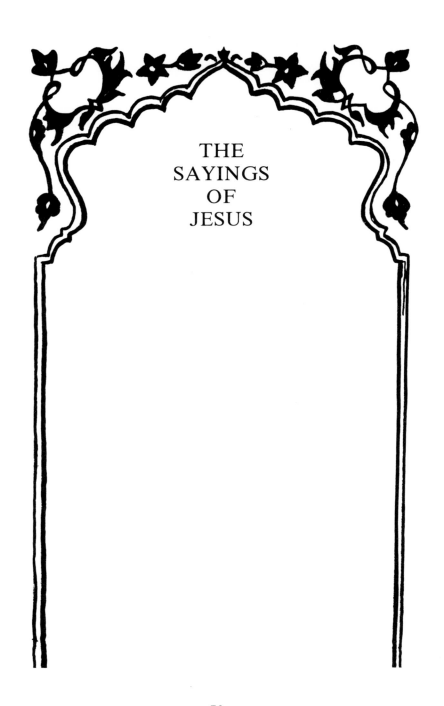

THE
SAYINGS
OF
JESUS

1) "Jesus said: 'Whoever possesses knowledge and applies it and instructs others, will be exalted in the celestial realm of the angels.' " — Ghazâli, Abu Hâmed, *op. cit.*, vol. I, p.46

2) "Jesus said: 'Good trees are abundant, but not all bear fruit, and fruit is plentiful, but not all of it is sweet. Now, knowledge is abundant, but not all of it is fruitful.' " — *Ibid.*, p. 105

3) "Jesus said: 'Do not impart wisdom to the uninitiated, for that is an injustice to wisdom, nor withhold it from the initiated, for that would be an injustice to them; be the doctor who is a friend and dispense the drug according to the pain.' " — *Ibid.*, p. 118

4) "Jesus said: 'Do not hang jewels about the necks of swine. Wisdom is finer than gems, and those who do not value it, are worse than swine' " — *Ibid.*, p. 172

5) "Jesus said: 'A plant can grow only in yielding earth, not on hard rock. In the same way, wisdom flourishes only in a humble heart, not one which is proud and unyielding.' " — *Ibid.*, vol. IV, p. 954

6) "Jesus said: 'The learned who are bad are like rocks damming the flow of a stream, serving to the benefit neither of the waterway nor the fields to which they are blocking access of the water. They are, moreover, like a sewage sump with a whitewashed cover, all shining on the outside, while its contents are just what it contains; and they are like graves which are blooming garden patches from without, while

within they are full of bones.' " — *Ibid.,* vol. I, p. 178

7) "Jesus said: 'How can anyone claim higher knowledge, knowing that he must pass on to the hereafter, yet expect something of this world? How can anyone claim higher knowledge and seek sage counsel only for preaching and not for practice?' " — *Ibid.,* p. 182

8) "Jesus said: 'One who teaches higher knowledge and does not practice its wisdom, is like a clandestine adulteress whose swelling condition betrays her to shame. Such a person who does not act on the precepts he knows, will be shamed by the Lord before all creation on the Day of Judgment.' " — *Ibid.,* p. 188

9) "Jesus said: 'God has declared that those who observe the canonical devotion will be saved, while those who perform supererogatory worship, will be drawn close to Him.' " — *Ibid.,* p. 78

10) "Jesus said: 'Whoever turns a beggar from his door, will not be visited by the angels for seven days.' " — *Ibid.,* vol. II, p. 217

11) "When Jesus was asked who had taught him *adab* (the etiquette of spiritual and social conduct), he replied: 'No one taught me. I saw the gracelessness of the ignorant and sought the reverse.' " — *Ibid.,* vol. III, p. 179

12) "Jesus said: 'Happy the one who foregoes the lust of the moment for the sake of what lies promised in the Beyond.' " — *Ibid.,* p. 181

13) "Jesus said: 'O company of disciples, keep your bellies empty that you may see the Lord in your hearts.' " — *Ibid.,* p. 207

14) "Jesus said: 'I prefer deprivation and despise

wealth.' When asked which epithet he liked best, he replied: 'Call me, "Pauper!" ' " — Makki, *Qut al-qolub,* vol. II., p.402

15) "Jesus said: 'The world was revealed to me as an old hag, bedecked with jewelry. I asked her how many husbands she had had, and she replied that she could not count them. I asked her whether they had died or she had divorced them. Her answer was, 'I murdered them every one'.

" ' "Alas," I cried, "so much the worse for the ones who remain. How is it that, in knowing about what has happened to their predecessors, who were slain each in his turn, they are not afraid?" ' " — Ghazâli, *op, cit.,* vol. IV, p.589

Shaikh 'Attâr in his *Oshtor-nâma (The Book of the Camel)* says:

The world is a foul and hunchback hag,
Murdering a million husbands a day.

Elsewhere, in his *Elâhi-nâma, (The Book of the Divine)* 'Attâr tells the following tale:

Though the level of Jesus, the Purified One, transcended paradise, still he desired to behold the world.

One day, while out walking, imbued with a divine radiance, Jesus perceived an old woman off in the distance. Hoary-haired and hunchbacked, she stood, her mouth drooped open in a toothless gaping stare. Her gloomy, sunken visage was pierced with eyes a livid blue, and a noxious odor emanated from her every pore. A motley frock she wore, but her heart was full of rancor and her head, of hostile spite. One hand was dyed a host of hues, the other drenched in blood. From every lock a buzzard's beak hung down, forming a frightful mask.

"Who are you," Jesus called out, on catching sight of her, "so cunning and so vile?"

"I am the realization of that desire you late conceived," the crone replied, "granted for your righteousness."

"Ah! So you are the squalid world!" he exclaimed.

"And that I am," she affirmed, "And how are you?"

"Why do you wear this veil?" he asked. "Why this parti-colored dress?"

"The veil is to keep my face from being seen, for if its hideousness were in view, who could stand to stay by me even for a moment? And this motley costume is to bedazzle men and lead them astray, for all who gaze on it are bewitched and enamored."

"You pit of disgrace," cried Jesus, "what means that blood-stained hand of yours?"

"Ah, prince of men," she said, "that comes from all the husbands I have slain."

"Now then, you drunken hag," said Jesus, "for what have you stained the other hand?"

"I use this dazzling allure," she said, "to seduce men into marrying me."

"Have you no mercy," queried Christ, "in murdering all these men?"

"What does mercy mean to me?" she countered. "All I know is shedding blood and seeing it flow."

"But you must have some semblance of tenderness," he insisted, "to encourage these victims with all your enticements."

"I have heard the name of 'mercy'," she replied, "but I have never applied it myself towards anyone. I stalk the ages and lure all I can into my trap. I turn all I catch into my disciples.

Jesus, amazed, gasped, "I'm appalled by such a mate! How can there be such deluded fools to chase after such a wanton strumpet?! Will they never learn from this accursed creature?! Can they never turn away and surrender to God? Oh, bemoan the folk who have missed the meaning and forsaken their faith, blind to the reality of the world."

With a few more words in this vein, that immaculate one turned his back on the world once and for all.

This delusive world is no more than a carcass, and your self worries it like a dog; there is no way for you to be unburdened of the dog, until it is fed up with this carcass-world. Only if you keep this dog leashed, can you be free; otherwise, you will find yourself harried by it day-in and day-out.

16) "Jesus said: 'Blessed is the one who surrenders as God's Book guides, for he will not die an oppressor.' " — Ghazâli, Abu Hamed, *op. cit.,* vol. IV., p.933

17 "Jesus said: 'Avoid what is prohibited, for it sows the seed of passion in the heart, and that is a great affliction.' " — *Ibid., vol. III.,* p. 278

18) "Jesus said: 'Devotion has ten degrees: the ninth is silence and the first, flight from people.' " — *Ibid.,* p. 304

19) "Jesus said: 'Whoever perennially lies, loses his beauty; and whoever quarrels with people, loses his human decency; and whoever is persistently despondent, becomes drawn and emaciated, and whoever behaves irritably, submits his soul to torture and misery.' " — *Ibid.,* p. 320

20) "John the Baptist asked Jesus what was the most difficult thing to bear. The latter replied: 'The Wrath of God.' 'Then,' asked John, 'what serves most to bring down God's Wrath?' 'Your own anger,' answered Jesus. 'And what brings on one's own anger?' asked John. Jesus said: 'Pride, conceit, vainglory and arrogance.' " — *Ibid.,* p. 383

21) "Jesus said: 'Do not make the world into a god, for it will make you its slave. Do not place your treasure in the hands of one who will squander it. One who possesses worldly wealth is haunted by fear of its spoiling, while there are no such qualms for the possessor of wealth from the Divine.' " — *Ibid.*, p. vol. IV, p.554

22) "Jesus said: 'O company of disciples! I have destroyed the world's attraction for you; so, after me do not succumb to involvement with it nor seek to restore it, for one of the evils of the world, is that people sin against God for its sake, not realizing that they must forswear it, in order to discover the hereafter. So, let the world go. Do not make much of it, knowing that the source of all sins is love of the world. How often an hour of lust has brought long grief for the one who has indulged in it!' " — *Ibid.*, p. 554

23) "Jesus said: 'I have toppled the world over on its face for you, and sat you on its back. So, neither kings nor wives should be entering into dispute with you. And let you not enter into dispute with kings, for as long as you have nothing to do with them and their world, they will not trespass against you. And as for wives, let you avoid involvement with them by engaging in prayer and fasting.' " — *Ibid.*

24) "Jesus said: 'The world is both seeking and sought. Thus, the world seeks out the seeker after the hereafter, to sate him with its provender, while the hereafter seeks out the seeker after the world, to bring death upon him, ensnaring him in its noose.' " — *Ibid.*

25) "Jesus said: 'Love of the world and love of the hereafter cannot be brought together in the heart of the believer, any more than fire and water can coexist in one place.' " — *Ibid.*, p. 559

26) "The disciples asked Jesus to guide them as to

what they might do to enter heaven. He told them: 'Keep forever silent'. They protested: 'We cannot do that!' 'Then,' said Jesus, 'say only what is good.' " — *Ibid.,* vol.III, p.303

27) "Jesus said: 'Who could build a house on the waves of the sea? That is what your world is, so do not be attached to it.' " — *Ibid.,* vol. IV, p. 563

28) "The disciples asked Jesus to teach them how to win God's love. He told them: 'Make the world your enemy, and God will befriend you.' " — *Ibid.*

29) "Jesus said: 'O company of disciples! Be less content with the world, in favor of faith, for the worldly are less content with faith, in favor of the world.' " — *Ibid.,* p.565

30) "Jesus said: 'O you who seek after worldly goods, in order to do good works, be aware that to renounce the world is more virtuous.' " — *Ibid.*

31) "Jesus said: 'The world and the hereafter are like two women which a man is trying to please at the same time; when one is pleased, the other is annoyed.' " — *Ibid.*

32) "Jesus said: 'The world is a bridge. Pass over it. Do not linger on it.' " *Ibid.,* p. 591

33) "Jesus said: 'The seeker after the world is like one who would drink from the sea; the more he drinks the more thirsty he becomes — until it kills him in the end.' " — *Ibid.,* p. 594

34) "Jesus's disciples asked him how it was that he could walk on water, while they could not. He countered: 'What is the worth of a *dinâr* and a *dirham*[1] to you?'

1. *Dinâr* and *dirham* are coins of the Middle East, the names reflecting Roman and Byzantine rule in the area before Islam, the former being the Arabicization of the Latin *denarius* and the latter, of the Greek *drachma*.

'Considerable,' they replied. 'To me they are the same as a clod of earth.' " — *Ibid.,* p. 640

35) "Jesus said: 'There are three objections to property. First, that it may not be obtained in an honest way.' 'But,' queried the disciples, 'what if it is gained correctly?' 'It may be spent dishonestly,' he replied. 'Then,' asked the disciples, 'what if it is spent correctly?' 'The very preoccupation with whether or not it is handled honestly or not, distracts one from remembering God,' he said, 'and this is a very painful matter, for the whole point of spiritual practice is the remembrance of God and reflection on His Majesty, and that requires a heart which is perfectly free of care.' " — *Ibid.,* p. 651

36) "Jesus said: 'Devote yourselves to obtaining that which fire cannot burn.' 'And what is that?' asked the disciples. 'Virtue,' he replied. — *Ibid.,* p. 672

37) "Jesus exclaimed: 'How is it that you come to me, dressed in ascetic robes, yet with the hearts of wolves? Put on the dress of kings and soften your hearts with dread and awe.' " — *Ibid.,* p. 975

38) "Jesus told his disciples: 'Whenever one of you should fast, he should smear grease on his hair and face and lips, so that no one is aware that he is fasting; and when he gives with his right hand, his left hand should not know what his right hand is doing; and when he prays, he should draw a curtain across the doorway; for God metes out His blessings as he apportions his provender.' " — *Ibid.,* p. 811

39) "Jesus said: 'Smart dress shows a prideful heart.' " — *Ibid.,* p. 982

40) "Hâreth Mohâsebi relates that Jesus said: 'O you learned ones with bad hearts! You fast and pray and give alms, yet you do not act on what the Scripture tells you, nor

do you practice what you preach. It is a bad precedent which you have chosen to follow, repenting in word and in wish, then pursuing your whims and caprices. What use is it that you make your skins clean, while your hearts remain impure? In truth, I urge you not to be as the sieve, out of which the refined flour flows and in which the chaff remains. With you, the wisdom pours from your mouths, while the deceit remains in your hearts.

" 'O slaves of the world! How can one attain to the hereafter, when his lust for the world still runs rampant, his desire for it still holds strong? I tell you in all truthfulness that your hearts weep at your deeds. In your prattling, your attention is towards the world, while you trample good works underfoot. I tell you in all truthfulness that you have despoiled the hereafter to the advantage of the world, for the interests of the world are closer, and therefore dearer, to you than those of the hereafter. Now, who do you think could be more miserly and retentive?

" 'O miserable wretches! How long can you go on claiming to light the way for those who are lost in the night, while you are mired down yourselves amongst the confused. The way you are, you even invite the worldly to give up the world, for *your* sake.'

" 'O wretches! What do you gain by putting a lamp on the roof of a dark house and leaving the house in darkness and terror. It hardly suffices that knowledge hangs on your lips, while your hearts are hollow and fearful.

" 'O bondsmen of the world! You have neither the virtue of devoted servants nor the generosity of free spirits. Be aware that the world for you will quickly be hurled from its pedestal, flung down on its face and toppled over mightily, and sin will seize you by the forelock, and knowledge will thrust you before the Requiter, naked and alone; and he will make your wrongs known to you, and mete out the retribution for your evil-doing.' " — *Ibid.*, p. 725

41) "Jesus said: 'The vision of anyone who does not

ponder the lessons that come to him is just idle reflection, and any expression which does not issue out of consciousness of God is empty triviality. For the one who contemplates in order to gain insight and speaks out in order to find someone of heart or turn a neglecter into a rememberer, his vision and utterance are all worship; while for one who looks through the eyes of passion or speaks with the tongue of ignorance or listens with the ears of caprice, all his activity is nothing more than toying about with the insidious trifles of the world.' " — *Aurâd al-ahbâb,* p.190

42) "It is related that the Prophet recounted how one of the disciples informed Jesus, son of Mary, of his father's death, requesting his permission to go and bury his father. Jesus replied: "Let the dead bury the dead. You follow me.' " — Solami, *Jawâme' âdâb as-sufiyah*

43) "Jesus said: 'My dress is wool[1] and my bread is fear of God; my diet is hunger and my lamp at night, the moon; my shelter from the cold, the sun, and the sustaining fruit of my life, that which sprouts from the earth as fodder for beasts; night and day pass for me alike, and of science I have no knowledge; yet no one is richer than I.' " — Abu Bakr Muhammad ebn 'Abdo'l-Karim, *op. cit.,* p.261

44) "Jesus told his disciples: 'Many a lamp has been extinguished by the wind, and many a devotee, ruined by pridefulness and conceit.' " — *Ibid.,* p. 200

45) "Jesus said: 'I tell you in all honesty and assurance that just as you humble yourselves, so will you be raised up and magnified; and just as you act with compassion, so will you be treated with mercy; and just as you rise to the needs of people, so will God tend to your needs.' " — *Ibid.*

---

1. 'Wool' in Arabic is *suf*, the most likely source for the word *sufi*.

46) "Jesus was asked: 'Why do you not build a house for yourself?' He replied: 'I have no interest in occupying myself with something with which I shall not be associated till the end of time.' " — Ansâri, *Tafsir-e 'erfâni,*vol.I, p.557

"Your sole peer in the sun," someone praised Jesus,
Mary's son, "Why don't you build
Yourself a house or home?"
"I'm not a lunatic. I'm not mad,"
Replied Christ, "to convey such baggage to eternity;
I have no need for such paraphernalia."
Whatever provisions won't further your way
Are vain and empty, be you prince or pauper.
                                    — 'Attâr, *Mosibat-nâma*

47) Jesus exclaimed to his people: 'How fine it would be to bring water and fire together!' 'O spirit of God!'[1] they cried, 'Explain further!' So he said: 'Reduce what you have on earth, that your deeds may not turn out fruitless." — Hamadhâni, *Nâmahâ,* p.455

48) "Jesus was asked what was the hardest thing to endure in the world. He replied, 'God's Wrath'. Then they queried, 'How can one be spared it?' And he answered, 'By breaking one's anger and controling one's temper.' — Rumi, *Fihe ma fihe,* (Foruzânfar), p.233

"What's the most difficult thing in existence to bear?"
someone inquired of Jesus.
"Hardest of all is the Wrath of God';
answered Christ.
Hell even quakes in awe,
As we tremble before it,"
"So what refuge from His wrath exists?"
he queried.

---

1. 'Spirit of God', translation of *Ruho'llâh,* an epithet given in Islam to Jesus as prophet. The reader is referred to the discussion on pp. 15 and 16 under the title *The Father of Jesus.*

"Abandon your anger, renounce your rage
The instant it appears," counseled Christ.

49) "It is related of Jesus that he said: 'O company of disciples! You fear to sin, while we prophets fear unbelief.' " — Ghâzali, *op. cit.*, vol.IV., p.172

50) "Jesus the prophet said: 'If you bear with the talk of a fool, you will benefit ten times over.' " Râzi, *Marmuzât-e asadi,* p.114

51) "Jesus the prophet said: 'The Lord granted me the power to bring the dead to life and make the blind to see and the congenitally deaf to hear, but He did not give me the power to cure a fool.' " — *Ibid.,* p. 115

52) "It is said of Jesus that he exhorted: 'O people of wisdom! Give advice as a doctor prescribes, dispensing drugs where they are beneficial and withholding them where they do harm. Do not dispense wisdom to the uninitiated, for you would only make a fool of yourself; nor withhold it from those who are worthy, for that would be unjust of you; and do not reveal your secrets to just anyone, for you would only put yourself to shame.' " — Shirâzi, *Tarâ'eq al-haqâ'eq,* vol.I, p.60)

53. "Said Jesus, son of Mary: 'You work for the world, heedless that your daily bread is provided for, without that effort; yet you do not labor for the hereafter, the benefits of which cannot be reaped without your working for it. Woe upon you, learned ones of bad hearts, who enjoy ill-gotten gains and turn efforts to bad ends. The time is at hand, when the doer will be called to account for his deeds, with which he is so pleased. Indeed, the time is nigh, when he will emerge from the straits of this world — and plunge into the darkness of the grave! How can one call oneself 'learned' in religion, on the way leading to one's reckoning in the hereafter, and yet be content with the world, preferring that

which is harmful to one, over that which is to one's benefit?!' "— *Ibid.,* vol.I, p.339

54. "When Jesus was asked by the disciples: 'With whom should we keep company?' he replied, 'With those whose association causes you to remember God.' " — *Ibid.,* p.428

55. "Jesus said: 'One cannot enter the spiritual world beyond the heavens and the earth, until one has been born again.' " — Hamadhâni, *Tamhidât*, p.12

The point here is that the person who emerges from his mother's womb, perceives only this world, while one who emerges out of himself, sees beyond this world. Hence, two births are necessary for every individual.

56) "Jesus said: 'A tear shed by one who has transgressed, quenches the fire of God's Wrath.' " — Ghazâli, Ahmad, *Resâla'i dar mau'eza* p.84

STORIES
RELATING TO
JESUS
IN
SUFI
BOOKS

1— THE DREAM WHICH HASAN EBN 'ALI HAD OF JESUS

"Hasan ebn 'Ali[1] dreamed one night that he saw Jesus son of Mary, whom he asked, 'As I would like to obtain a ring, what should I have inscribed upon it?' Jesus replied, 'Put, "There is no god but God, the true and clear Sovereign". That is what is said at the end of the Gospel.' "
— Qoshairi, *Resâla* p.719

2— JESUS'S DISCOURSE ON THE 'SOUL' OF GOD

"One day a great scholar came to see Maulânâ Jalâlo'd-Din Rumi.[2] Wishing to test Rumi, he set about posing several questions, of which one was: 'Is it possible for God to have a soul? If so, how is one to understand this in the light of the verse *(Âle 'emrân [The Family of 'Imrân]*, 185) which reads, "Every soul will taste of death", when compared to the text of the verse *(Mâ'edah [The Table Spread]*, 116), in which Jesus declares, "You know what is in my soul, whereas I know not what is in Yours", in which 'soul' is ascribed to the ineffable Godhead? Are not these two statements contradictory?'

"Rumi replied, 'One must interpret the expression, 'I know not what is in Your Soul,' to mean 'in Your Knowledge and Your Essence.' " — Aflâki, *Manâqeb al-'ârefin*, vol.I, p.269

---

1. Ḥasan ebn 'Ali (d. 49/669), the elder son of 'Ali ebn Abi Ṭâleb, cousin of the Prophet, and Fâṭima, daughter of Moḥammad. He is called 'Emâm Ḥasan' by the Shi'a Moslems, who regard him as the successor to the imamate of his father.
2. Maulânâ Jalâlo'd-Din Rumi (d. 672/1273) was a great master, as well as endowed poet, having written the *Mathnawi*, six volumes of rhyming couplets, to instruct his disciples and followers of the Path in succeeding generations, and the *Diwân-e shams* to inspire devotees on the Path.

91

3— JESUS APPEARS IN A DREAM TO MOHAMMAD EBN KHAFIF[1]

"Abu 'Abdo'llâh Modammad ebn Khafif of Shiraz relates that he saw Jesus in a dream, and said to him, 'O Spirit of God![2] The Qoran states that you have told the people that you could tell them what they ate and what they had stored up in their houses *(Äle 'emrân,* 49).' Ebn Khafif went on to say: 'Jesus replied, "The Lord's Word is the Truth."[3] Then I said, "Can you tell me what Abo'l-Qâsem Saffâr had last night for dinner, as well as what he has put away in reserve?" Jesus told me, "He ate dates and moist cheese; then put some of it away." The following day, I got up and went over to see my neighbor, and told him, "Go and get out those dates you've stored away, and let's eat them!" He wanted to know how I knew about them; so I told him the story.' " — Baqli, *Ruzbehân-nâma,* p.10

4— JESUS'S PATCHWORK CLOAK OF WOOL

"By reliable account, Jesus, son of Mary, had a patchwork cloak, which he wore when he ascended into heaven. One of the masters of the Path once said that he had seen him in a dream, wearing that same old patchy woolen cloak, and that beams of light shone from every patch. He explained, 'I cried, "O Christ, how come these beams of light from your dress?" And he replied, "These are the rays of my misery. Every rip and tear which I had to mend, the Good Lord turned to light, representing all the pangs of suffering which have stung my heart." ' " — Hojwiri, *Kashf al-mahjub* p.56

1. Abu 'Abdo'llâh Mohammad ebn Khafif Shirâzi (d. 982 AD) was a great saint of Shiraz in the south of Iran, important in the school of mystics who interpreted Sufism within the context of the Ash'arite school of theology. He was a master of Abu Nasr Sarrâj, whose *Ketâb al-loma' fe't-tasawwof* is a major exposition of Sufi doctrine.
2. See discussion of this epithet of Jesus *Ruho'llâh* under the title *The Father of Jesus* (pp.15-16)
3. This is a translation of the standard phrase with which a chanter of the Qoran closes his recitation *Sadaqa'llâho'l-'aliyo'l-'azim).*

5— DESIRE FOR BREAD

"It is related of Jesus that he stood in supplicatory prayer to his Lord for sixty days without eating. Eventually the desire for bread came upon his heart, and his praying stopped short. Jesus sat down and wept in grief at the loss of his prayerful concentration, when suddenly he felt the presence of a spiritual master by his side. Jesus cried, 'O saint of God, pray for me, for I was in a state of prayer, when the thought of bread intruded on my mind, and that state was cut off.' The master replied, 'O Lord, since I have come to know you, if ever the desire for bread should come upon my heart, may You never grant me pardon.' " — Ghazâli, Abu Ḥâmed, *op.cit.*, vol.III, p.230

6— VIRTUOUS WORDS

"A pig once passed Jesus by, and he greeted it, saying, 'Pass in peace.' 'O Spirit of God,' said those who were around him, 'why do you speak to a pig in this way?' He replied, 'I find it unpleasant to accustom my toungue to bad words.' "

— *Ibid.*, p. 326

7— THE HOMELESSNESS OF JESUS

"It is recorded that Jesus was once caught in a violent thunderstorm, driving him to seek shelter. He spied a tent from afar and made for it, only to discover that there was a woman inside. Fleeing away again, he ran until he caught sight of a cave in the mountainside. When he entered it, he found a lion within. Placing his hand on the lion's head, he called out, 'O Lord, everything has a place of its own; only I have none!'

"A revelation came to him, whereby the Lord declared, 'Your place is in the bosom of My Mercy. I shall make you a match with a hundred houris, created with the might of My Hand; and I shall provide festivities lasting four thousand years, each year as long as the entire life of the earth; and I shall dispatch heralds to proclaim to the pious of the earth that they are invited to the wedding feast of the most devout of all, Jesus, son of Mary.' " —*Ibid.,* vol. IV p. 560

8— JESUS WITHOUT SHELTER

"It is recounted that Jesus was wandering in the desert, when a sudden storm blew up, so that he took shelter in a nearby cave, the lair of a caracal, until the storm should let up. A revelation came to him, whereby the Lord told him to quit the caracal's den, because his presence was disturbing the animal's cubs.

"He exclaimed, 'O Lord, even the beasts of the field[1] have a refuge, but the son of Mary has none! Neither hearth nor home has he, no shelter, no roof over his head, nor any place or status.'

"The Lord replied, 'The caracal has a home, indeed, but it has no Beloved to drive it from its home, such as you have. What is there to regret about having a Beloved with such grace as to drive you out, singling you out of all creatures to bestow upon you such a blessing. It is worth — nay, has even greater value than — a thousand times a hundred thousand heavens and earths, worlds and hereafters, Thrones and Stools[2] — all the panoply of the universe put together.' " — Rumi, *Fihe mâ fihe* (Foruzânfar), pp.41-2

1. The actual meaning of this expression is 'jackal', being a translation of the Arabic *ebn âwâ.* Rumi, in his Persian prose text of the *Fihe mâ fihe,* has left this phrase in the original Arabic of the source from which he has taken the anecdote, in order to preserve the pun expressed in it, for *ebn âwâ* literally means 'son of shelter', which provides a verbal foil for *ebn maryam* ('son of Mary'), besides carrying over a further play on words relating to the animal offspring, the caracal's cubs.
2. The Divine Throne *('arsh)* and Stool *(korsi)* represent successively in descending order two of the highest stations on the Way towards human perfection, approaching the Godhead. In Sufi philosophy, the Throne stands for the Universal Spirit *(ruh al-koll)* and the Stool for the Universal Soul *(nafs al-koll).* The throne is further defined in Jorjâni's *Definitions,* cited in the author's forthcoming several-volume *Treasury of Sufi Terminology,* vol. IV, as the realm from which the Divine ordinations governing the destiny of phenomena descend.

" 'Ammâr ebn Sa'd relates that Jesus arrived at a village where the inhabitants were all lying dead in the pathways and around the houses. 'O company of disciples,' he declared, 'this community has been destroyed by the Wrath of God; otherwise, they would have been properly buried.' 'O Spirit of God,' they urged, 'let us have news of what has happened to them!'

"So Jesus invoked God's Name, and a revelation came, whereby God told him to call out to the villagers after nightfall to obtain the answer.

"When night came, Jesus went up on a hilltop and hailed the dead populace, and one of the villagers answered up: 'At your service, O Spirit of God!' Jesus asked what had happened to them. The reply came: 'We spent a peaceful night and woke up in the morning to find ourselves in the pit of hell.'

"Jesus asked why, 'Because we loved the world,' came the answer, 'and obeyed the behest of sinful people.' 'In what way did you love the world?' queried Jesus. 'The way a child loves its mother,' was the reply. 'Whenever it came to us, we were happy, and whenever it went away, we became sad and wept.'

"Then Jesus asked, 'Why do your comrades not speak up?' 'Harsh and brutal angels have clamped red-hot bits on their mouths,' the voice answered. 'Then how is it that you are able to speak?' countered Jesus. 'I was not of them,' said the other, 'even though I was with them. When the torment descended, I remained amongst them. At present, I am at the edge of hell, not knowing whether I shall be saved or cast down into the infernal depths.'

"At this point, Jesus turned to his disciples and told them: 'Eating barley bread with rock salt and wearing sackcloth and sleeping on dunghills in squalor is more than enough to assure one's well-being in this world and the next.' " — Ghazâli, *op.cit.,* vol. IV, p.562

10— JESUS AND THE DEVIL (EBLIS)

"The Devil appeared before Jesus and told him to say, 'There is no god but God.' Jesus replied, 'The words are right, but I am not going to repeat them when you tell me to!' " — *Ibid.,* vol. III, p. 88

Ghazâli points out, by way of commentary, that the Devil's work of deception can don the most virtuous of cloaks, his ruses of this nature being endless.

11— JESUS AND THE DEVIL

"It is related that Jesus was lying with a stone under his head as a pillow, when the Devil passed by and mocked him, saying, 'You still desire something in the world, I see.'

"Jesus took the stone out from under his head and flung it at the Devil, crying, 'Take this and the whole world with it!' " — *Ibid.,* p. 99

Sanâ'i, in his *Hadiqat al-ḥaqiqah (The Enclosed Garden of the Truth),* provides a longer and more involved version of the foregoing anecdote:

"I've read in historical works that one night Jesus wandered out into the desert. An hour passed and, feeling fatigued, he looked for a place to rest. He found a stone lying before him in the dust, so he put it under his head as a pillow and fell quickly asleep. After an hour's sleep, he awoke to see Satan standing before him.

" 'You accursed and outcaste dog!' cried Jesus. Why have you come here to deceive me? This is hallowed ground, the abode of Jesus, the Immaculate. How can it accomodate you?'

" 'You're trespassing on my land,' the Devil replied, 'and troubling me. Why do you loiter in my realm? This ground, the kingdom of the world, is entirely my property. Why have you forcibly seized my lands? You make me cringe before your purity.'

" 'When did I ever trespass on your property?' Jesus asked. 'When did I ever bother you?'

" 'What about this stone then,' the Devil asked, which

you've taken as a pillow for yourself? Haven't you stolen it from the land?'

"Jesus picked up the stone and flung it away. Satan suddenly shrank and began to shrivel up.

" 'You've driven me off!' he cried, 'And freed yourself, as well. Both of us now are liberated. I won't trouble you any more, but leave my domain to me.' "

'Aṭṭâr narrates another version of this tale in his *Moṣibat-nâma (The Book of Affliction) p. 179):*

"Jesus, son of Mary, had fallen asleep, having laid his head to rest on a clod of earth. When he opened his eyes out of his slumber, he saw that Eblis, the Accursed, was standing before him.

" 'You abominable being!' Jesus cried. 'Why are you standing here?' "Eblis replied, 'That's *my* clod of earth you've used to cushion your head as a pillow! The whole world is, in fact, my fief — and that clearly includes that clod! As long as you intrude on my domain, you're subject to my tutelage. You're my disciple.'

"Jesus flung the clod at Eblis, and lay back to go back to sleep on the ground.

" 'Sleep well,' said Satan in conclusion.

Within the terracotta walls of the grave you'll rest;
Why match together now
    empty bricks and mortar?
If mortar can be made of the heart's tears,
Why cement brick to brick
    for the sake of the world?

12— REPROACH FOR BACKBITING ONE'S BROTHER

"Once Jesus asked his disciples what they would do if they happened on one of their brothers, sleeping with his private parts exposed.

"They replied, 'Why, we would cover them up, of course!'

" 'Well, in fact, you not only do not do that — you go about making the situation worse!'

" 'God forbid! Who would ever do such a thing!' they cried.

"Jesus told them, 'Every time you listen to gossip about your brother, then add to what the other person is saying in finding fault with him, expanding on what has been said, you have done just what I have said.' " — Kâshâni, *Mesbâh al-hedâyah* p.242

13— THE MAN WHO NEVER SINNED

"It is recounted that Jesus once went into the desert to pray for rain. When people gathered round, he said to them, 'Whoever has sinned, must go back.' Everyone went away, except one man. Jesus turned to this man and asked him, 'Have you never sinned?' The man replied, 'By God's Name, I know nothing of sin. Indeed, one day I was saying my prayers, when a woman passed by. My eye happened to fall upon her, so I plucked it out and cast it behind her.'

"Jesus then told him to pray. As soon as he began, clouds proceeded to gather. Rain began to fall — and a goodly downpour it was!" — Ghazâli, *op. cit.,* vol. II, p. 437

14— JESUS'S PRAISE OF A DOG'S WHITE TEETH

"Mâlek Dinâr relates that Jesus, son of Mary, out walking with his disciples, happened to pass by the carcass of a dog. 'Whew!' exclaimed the disciples. 'What a stench!' Jesus then paused to remark upon the shining whiteness of the creature's teeth. As the account goes, Jesus then proceeded to chastize his disciples, telling them not to speak ill of the poor dog and declaring, 'Say nothing about God's creatures except that which is in praise.' " — *Ibid.,* vol. III, p. 383

Nezâmi in his *Makhzan al-asrâr (The Treasure-trove of*

Mysteries) gives another version of this story:

"Once Jesus, the wanderer of the world, passed by a bazaar. On the side of the road, he spied the carcass of a dog, abandoned like Joseph in the well. A motley group of bystanders were gathered round, hovering over the carrion like vultures.

" 'What an awful stench!' one commented. 'The odor dims the mind like a lantern in the wind.' " 'That's not all,' another observed. 'The sight of it blurs the vision and makes me sick to my stomach.'

"The crowd of onlookers continued in this vein, venting their ill-will on the carcass. Jesus, when his turn came, declared, 'How beautiful are those teeth, displayed in the jaws!'

"The remaining bystanders, however, moved either by disgust or by mischief, carried on with their ridicule."

Overlook others' faults;
Disregard your own charity;
Turn your eyes inward
To contemplate yourself instead.

'Aṭṭar in his *Moṣibat-nâma* (p. 302) relates the story in another way:

A dog lay dead by the wayside,
Jaws open, on the earth outstretched.
A foul odor filled the air.
As Jesus passed by, he cried,
"How reverend this creature is!
What beauty in the whiteness of his teeth!"
Blind to odor, to ugliness,
He viewed only beauty.

If you're a seer of reality,
A true bondsman of Divinity,

Profess pureheartedness;
Look on all as one
Hue, color and sum.
Practice goodness and charity,
Kindness and fidelity;
God's gifts with gratitude
Repay like a devotee.
If you've any gnosis of Him,
Be indentured in God's service.
Receiving His gifts always
With gratitude.

Year in and year out
You thrive on His bounty,
Yet neglect to acknowledge
His graces with your gratitude.

15— THE PIOUS ELDER AND THE SINNER

"It is said that once, Jesus son of Mary, was out walking, accompained by one of the pious elders of the Children of Israel. Along came a notorious sinner, who joined them with head cast down and repentant heart. The sinner prayed, 'O Lord, have mercy upon me!', while the pious elder prayed, 'O Lord, bring me not together with this miscreant on the Day of Judgment!'

"The Lord sent down a revelation to Jesus, saying that He had answered both their prayers. 'I have rejected the pious elder,' he explained, 'and pardoned the sinner.' " — Qoshairi, *op. cit.,* p. 196

Now, Ghazâli gives a different version of the same story in his *Ehyâ al-'olum (Revival of the Religious Sciences):*

"There once was a highwayman, it is said, who roved and pillaged the towns of the Israelites for a good forty years. Jesus encountered him one day when he was out walking with one of his disciples, one of the most pious worshippers amongst the Children of Israel.

"The thief was moved to say to himself, 'This is a prophet of God, who is passing by, and that is one of his disciples. How fine it would be if I were just to approach them and make us a threesome!'

"So, he approached the pair and sought to fall in step beside the pious disciple, rebuking himself all the while for his temerity in desiring to be close to a man of such righteousness. No sooner had the disciple become aware of his presence than he began to mutter to himself that he should not be seen with this man walking beside him; so he moved aside and stepped in closer to Jesus, so as to be seen in the latter's company, with the brigand bringing up the rear.

"God sent down a revelation to Jesus, saying, 'Tell them both that they must begin anew. All their deeds of the past have been erased. Even the good works of the disciple have been eradicated because of his pridefulness. Likewise have the thief's bad deeds been wiped clean because of his humble self-deprecation.'

"Accordingly, Jesus informed the two of God's decree. Thereupon, the brigand joined Jesus in his wanderings and became accepted in the company of his disciples."

The poet Sa'di has still a further rendition of this tale, in the chapter on 'Humility' in his epic-length *Bustân:*

I've heard them recite —
*   those experts in traditional theology —*
a tale of a sinner and a saint,
*   alive in the era of the Messiah.*
A villain so infamous, so decadent, the devil
*   even was ashamed of his acquaintance;*
his life a labor in vain,
*   squandered in superfluities, an aggravation*

to every heart, a coarse mind
　　devoid of reason or elegance;
nurtured on impurity, his belly full
　　of unlawful viands. Oppression his profession,
his honor stained with depravity,
　　folly-filled ears heedless to exhortation,
his wayward feet led astray,
　　erring, while wending his way.

Hated by men like a famine,
　　his evil was hailed from afar,
like the harvest moon.
　　Passions ravaged his soul,
lust sapped his resources.
　　His excesses had blackened every sheet —
no line to inscribe some further fault
　　was left in the ledger of his acts,
nor a grain of virtue to his name.
　　Urge-driven to sin, a votary of desire
and prisoner of passion,
　　he wallowed dazed in a drunken
stupor day and night.

The saint-errant, Jesus, I heard then
　　was wandering across a desert waste.
There, among the foothills he encountered
　　a devotee's ascetory.
From his promontory of solitude
　　the ascetic descended, love-drawn to embrace
his Messiah's feet with kisses,
　　prostrating his brow in the dust.
From the desert's outskirts, the sinner, too,
　　object of fate's inverted star, was drawn
like the mad amor of a moth
　　to that flame's foot, Christ's light.
Chagrined, self-condemned, he entreated
　　forgiveness for his nights of forgetfulness;
chastened, shamefaced as a pauper

begging before a prince;
clouds of rainy grief wept
    from his eyes' skies:
"...Alas, my life's labor lost,
    the precious assets I've amassed
all flown to the wind.
    May nobody be alive like me;
like me, my death far excels my life.
    To die as a baby is best, at least
the infant dead are liberated
    and needn't bemoan vain old age."
Tears flowed freely down his face,
    crestfallen, brow bowed in shame,
moaning, "O Worldmaker, O Creator,
    absolve my sins, lest they scourge
me like demon-consorts."[1]

The aging sinner loitered upset
    on one end of the plain,
beseeching God's succour,
    while the arrogant ascetic stood apart,
brows raised in censorious disdain
    at the professed 'profligate', as if
to say: 'Who's this miscreant to companion us?
    Ugh! This fool supposes himself fitting
for the company of Jesus and me!
    Facedown in the Fire you've fallen,
steeped in wantonness up to your neck;
    your life, only dedicated to depravity,
What positive virtue can your decadence generate?
    How can anyone so God-forlorn
Walk next to the Messiah and me?

---

1. Sa'di has the sinner here invoke the Qoran's theology that evil deeds themselves generate a 'devil-mate' which aligns itself with the wrong-doer. The reference is to *Zokhrof (Ornaments of Gold)*, 36-38:
    "Whosoever's vision is dim in remembering the All-Merciful, We assign a devil as a comrade. Look! From God's way they're thwarted, though they account themselves well-directed. Until at last to Us he arrives, and cries (to his comrade), 'Alas, that between me and you were two horizons' distance — an evil comrade."

Like an evil star you haunt me.
I'm troubled, tormented lest
    your fire-filled being enkindle me, as well.
O Lord, at the Resurrection,
    upon the Judgment Day,
don't seat me knee-to-knee with him!'

The signs of Glory struck his being,
    yet Jesus only heard an angelic epiphany
amidst the ascetic's ignorant curses:
    'Both the fool and the wiseman I accept',
the Divine Call came. 'Both petitions I endorse,
    but the poseur of piety gets sent
straight to hell, and the other,
    blackguard and profligate, I elevate
to heaven in My Grace;
    for he turned to Me repentant,
wept, was chastened and sobered by
    his darkened days, the opportunities cast away.
I cannot cast out
    from the chancel of My Mercy
anyone who seeks Me with such
    self-avowed wretchedness.
But if the puritan dogmatist thinks he's
    defiled by the sinner in heaven's synod...
Very well, tell him not to worry.
    Let the self-proclaimed saint
go to hell and the debauchee
    he despises, go to paradise.
For one rent his soul in remorse,
    seared in conscience, scalded
himself with tears, while the other
    relied on his personal ascetic devotion.
If only be knew:
    in the court of the Opulent,
helplessness excels pride,
    contrition outshines egoism.

The clothes of pride are pretty,
but the underwear is filthy.
On this threshold
poverty and contrition
serve you better than
self-adoration or devotion.
Your ego's assessment informs you,
'I'm virtuous,'
but watch out! Godliness
and egoism are opposites.
Cut your machismo and bravado,
if you're a man.
No every royal rider
strikes the ball off the turf.
The egoist is as artless as an onion,
all peel, all ignorance,
presuming to be pithy himself
as a pistachio.
Obedience like this is all inane
Go, confess your devotion has holes in it;
ask that your sloth be absolved.
It simply doesn't matter whether
you're a profligate, fortune wasted away,
or painstaking ascetic full of vain mortification.
Work on piety;
practice sincerity, purity, austerity.....
But don't pretend to transcend
Mohammad.
For a fool alone adores the Creator
but is unloving to creatures
and he'll never savor the fruit
of the Tree of Devotion.
The wise all have their adages,
pronounced for posterity;
from Sa'di
learn by heart one maxim alone:
The soul-mortified sinner,
brooding on God,

is better than the canting ascetic,
affecting piety.

16— JESUS AND JOHN

"It is well known that John the Baptist never laughed in all his life and that Jesus never cried, for the former was in a state of contraction and the latter in one of expansion.[1]

"Once they met each other, and John asked Jesus if he was immune from God's Wrath, and Jesus countered by asking John if he had no hope of the Divine Mercy, concluding with the words: 'Neither will your weeping affect eternal ordination nor my mirth change the grand design." — Hojwiri, *op. cit.,* p. 490

17— JESUS'S SELF-ABNEGATION

"It is said that the sole worldly possession of Jesus was a cup from which he drank water. One day he chanced to see a man drinking water from his cupped hand. Thenceforth, he did without the cup, declaring, 'Till now I was unaware that God had bestowed a cup upon me.' " — Ansâri,*op. cit.,* vol. I, p. 389

18— JESUS THE DESTITUTE

"They say that when the destitute are summoned on the Day of Judgment, they will claim their due from the Lord on the plea that He had created them impoverished, so that they could not serve Him properly. At this point, Jesus will be brought forward, as one who came into the world and left it without a penny to his name, so that he should be the one to judge." — *Ibid.*

19— JESUS AND HIS DONKEY

"Jesus had a grey donkey which never went more than

---

1. Contraction *(qabḏh)*and expansion *(baṣt)* are two involuntary spiritual states which descend on the heart from God. As the Qoran states: "God contracts and He expands."

two leagues a day. Such was Jesus's pity that one night he made two hundred trips to bring the beast water, so much did he attend to the animal. When the obstinate creature refused to drink, Jesus, out of concern, stayed up all night.

"The following day, the disciples became curious about their master's mysterious vigil.

"Jesus told them, 'He has no tongue with which to voice his needs. When he is thirsty, it is hardly my place to sleep. He has carried me around all day; if he does not drink, I have the Almighty to answer to for my shame. How can I sleep with my thirst quenched, while he has not drunk and has no way of telling me?'

"Nobility is no more than humble service to the Creator and kindness to all creatures."

— Auhadi Marâghi Esfahâni,
Diwân

20— JESUS AND A LYING COMPANION

"Jarir cites Laith as relating that once there was a man who fell in with Jesus on his travels. Going on together for a time, they reached a stream, where they sat down to have a bite of breakfast. They had three loaves between them, giving them one apiece, which they consumed, and one left over. Jesus rose and went over to the stream to drink. When he returned he found the remaining loaf missing. Asking who had taken it, he was told, 'I do not know.'

"So they went on, until they spied a doe with two fawns. Jesus called for one of the fawns and it came, offering itself to be slain. Jesus roasted the slaughtered beast and presented it for the two of them to eat. After they had partaken of it, Jesus called out to the consumed fawn, 'In the Name of the Lord, arise!' And it rose up, whole, and walked away. Then Jesus turned to the other man and cried, 'In the Name of that Lord who has shown you this sign, I ask you who has taken that loaf?' Again the man replied, 'I do not know.'

"They walked on, until they came to a river. Jesus took the man's hand and they both set out walking on the water across that river. When they reached the other side, again Jesus asked, 'In the Name of that Lord who has shown you this sign, who has taken that loaf?' And again the man answered, 'I do not know.'

"Proceeding on, they arrived at a desert. Jesus scooped up a handful of earth and cried, 'By God's command, become gold!' And it turned to gold, which Jesus divided into three parts, saying this third is mine, this one yours, and the remainder for the one who took the loaf. Straightaway, the man spoke up, telling him, 'I took it!' Thereupon, Jesus gave him the whole lot and left him.

"As the man proceeded through the wilderness, he met two men, who, on discovering the gold with him, sought to kill him for it, but he pleaded for them to share it three ways, whereupon they agreed, sending one of their number on to a nearby village to bring food. The one going to the village, set to thinking along the way, 'Why should I share the gold with the others? I shall simply poison this food and kill them off.' And so he put poison in the food.

"In the meantime, the other two were thinking, 'Why should we give up a third to him, when we can keep it for ourselves?' So they agreed to kill him, when he returned. Once they had done that, they ate the poisoned food and promptly died themselves, leaving the gold abandoned in the desert.

"Jesus came by and saw what had taken place. He turned to those who were with him and said, 'This is the way of the world. So beware!' " — Ghazâli, *op. cit.,* vol. IV, p.750

'Attâr provides similar version of the above in his *Moṣibat-nâma* (pp. 169-171).

21— JESUS'S REACTION TO DEATH
_____

Though joy to Jesus was like second nature,
*   still he trembled when he remembered death.*
Though endowed with warmheartedness

108

and blessed with expansiveness,
he shook in awe from head to foot,
drenched in a bloody sweat,
mortified by his own mortality.

— 'Attâr,
Mosibat-nâma, p. 94

22— JESUS AND THE SLEEPER

"Jesus went into a cave and found a man lying there, sound asleep.

" 'Rise and to get work!' Jesus exhorted the man. 'Accomplish something; provide the wherewithal for yourself! The world goes by!'

"The work I've done,' the man attested, 'is worth the two worlds. I've secured myself a dominion until eternity.'

" 'But what's your work, O pilgrim?' Jesus inquired.

" 'The world to me,' the man retorted, 'is but a piece of straw, a crust of bread, which I would fling to the dogs, like a bone. I've been free of the world for a long time now. I'm not a baby any more to play with Divine gratuities.

" 'What is the world, its pastimes and pageantry, to me? What are its gratuities, what is its gaiety, to me? Of such negligence, such heedlessness, I'm free.'

" 'When he heard this rejoinder, Jesus said, 'Sleep free. Go, do as you will; since the world cannot bother you, you've accomplished everything at once.' "

— *Ibid.,* p. 147

23— JESUS AND THE MAN WHO DESIRED AN ATOM OF LOVE

"As Jesus was traveling across a plain, he saw a man who had made a retreat for himself there. It was a secluded haunt with a running natural spring and an oratory for prayer, and it was surrounded by green shrubbery.

"My dear God-fearing ascetic,' Jesus addressed the man, 'why do you seclude yourself so?'

" 'Devotion has been my life-long labor,' the man replied, 'but my one overwhelming desire has still not been granted by God.'

" 'And what is that?' Jesus inquired.

" 'To drink one draught of Divine Love,' confessed the ascetic.

"Jesus prayed that his desire be gratified, then rose and continued on his way. It was granted by God's grace.

"Once again, in the course of his wanderings, Jesus happened to pass by the same spot and saw that the retreat was in a shambles, and the sand had blown over it. The oasis had dried up and the man's prayer-niche had crumbled to pieces.

" 'O Lord,' Jesus petitioned, 'where has this man gone? How has this place become ruined like this? Explain this tragedy to me.'

" 'You will find him on a certain mountaintop,' God revealed to Jesus, 'himself a mountain of grief from head to foot.'

"Finding the mountain, Jesus saw the man with his lips all shriveled and his face pale and parched. Jesus was dismayed and astounded; the man appeared like a living corpse. His hair was crackling with anguish, and the desert dust played freely over his face. He was caked with dirt and blood; his eyes seemed like bottomless pits. When Jesus hailed him with greetings of peace, he received no salutation in reply.

"Jesus was then confided this revelation by God: 'Such was his own entreaty. He desired an atom of Love. When I gave it to him, he gave up everything. He ceased to care about himself. He was obliterated, became utterly helpless. Had I poured one atom more of My Glory upon him, he would have been shattered into a thousand pieces.' "

"An atom even, in Love, is too much;
Conceit in Love is unbefitting.
Besides Love itself,
Whatever else subsists, is

Like an idol-temple
Within the Ka'ba.
When alien names from the heart
Are extirpated, the veils
From the Loved One's visage are raised.

—'Attâr, *Mosibat-nâma,*
pp. 278-9

24— JESUS AND EBLIS

"When Jesus saw Eblis occupied with prayer and devotion, he was curious about the intentions of the Accursed One.

" 'Devotion is a habit with me,' explained the Devil, 'a kind of lifelong protocol to pay for my sins.'

"O fallen angel!' retorted Jesus, 'again you've gone astray, mistaken God's way — displaying your usual ignorance!'

* * *

"Whatever is mere ingrained habit is no more than illusion; all religion which is mere ritual is just sham. This world was consigned, from pole to pole, to Satan long ago; yet here and there you wander about trying to steal it back for yourself.

"Whoever steals the Devil's merchandise, it's clear what his condition will be tomorrow. It's the Devil's bazaar, this world far and wide; its profits and purchases overseen by Eblis himself.

"In this bazaar of trite materialism if Satan's instigation were not in play, buisness everywhere would wane. He is the lodestar of every bazaar. Were Eblis absent, the world's work would wither away." — *Ibid.,* p. 122

25— JESUS AND THE WATER-POT

"Jesus once stopped to drink from a brook of sweet running water and found its taste sweeter than rosewater. A man came along with an earthenware pot and knelt by the stream's edge to fill it; then he offered the water to Jesus. Hardly had Jesus's lips touched the rim when he drew back in surprise at the briny bitter taste that met his mouth.

" 'O Lord,' cried Jesus, 'the same water is in the stream that is in the vessel, yet one is sweet as honey while the other is brackish and unsavory. How does this come to be?'

"It was the vessel itself that answered Jesus, saying, 'I am aged, a man of ancient days. Beneath this heavenly vault, I've been fashioned over and over a thousand times into pot and cask and mortar. And even were I to be molded over a thousand times again into a drinking vessel, you would still, in imbibing my contents, taste the acrid flavor of death in me. The taste of me is bitter and rancid, for death itself is putrid.

" 'From the vessel of mortality,' the pot spoke on, 'quaff the wisdom of refraining from fashioning yourself into a beaker of neglect. If you fail to discover who you are when you are alive, how can you hope to know yourself when you are dead? Your quest unconsummated while in life, your death is no more than a loss. Though born a man, you die unmanly. A hundred thousand veils shroud the Sufi's vision. How can he ever find himself?' "

— 'Attâr, *Manṭeq aṭ-ṭair,*
p.157

26— JESUS REVILED BY THE JEWS

"Once Jesus the Pure, while passing through an alleyway, was the butt of insults hurled by a crowd of mockers amongst the Jews. Yet he only smiled at their curses and offered prayers up in their behalf, returning their spiteful looks with benign compassion.

" 'Does not this slander affect you,' someone asked him, 'while you go on blithely praying for the mockers?'

" 'Every heart,' replied Jesus kindly, 'lives out and acts out the qualities contained within the soul of that person. Every wave of the sea of the soul, washing up against the shore, exposes the flotsam and jetsam of that ocean's contents. When you expire, breathing your last, all your contents are laid bare. A man's soul is truly weighed when blind fools direct the scenario of his life.

" *'Now, today,* you must bring your heart to imbibe the grief which tomorrow will bestow upon you in any event. Enkindle your heart here and now with a soul-scorching fear of this eventual grief. Die you must — and die again and again, a hundred times over — or else you cannot traverse this path. You must maintain an inward rapture, however much the fire scourges you, searing down from the empyrean realm. Thus, in dying expanded with joy, you will emerge more ardent than the fire itself.' "

— 'Attar, *Elâhi-nâma,*

pp. 235-6

Another version of this anecdote is recounted by Mohammad Lâhiji in his *Sharh-e golshan-e râz,* p.718. A prose rendition of Lâhiji's verse is provided here:

"With his pure and saintly spirit, Jesus valued a hundred worldly kingdoms less than a grain of barley. He set forth one day, in the company of a few stalwart and able companions, to travel the earth. Whenever he was harried along the way, it was his custom to reply with mildness, offering a prayer in behalf of those who accosted him. According to tradition, wherever he went, Jesus brought out the good in all that occurred to him, however inauspicious it might seem to be.

"His friends might protest: 'How is it that you undergo such indignity, yet pray God to pardon those who inflict it upon you?'

"Straightforward was his reply: 'One only reveals what is inside of one.'

"The truth of this assertion is symbolized by the parable of the rose and the thorn. However much he is stung by the barbs, Jesus, simply blossoms forth with a benign smile."

"Armed with a staff, a snake-charmer was crouching beside a snake-hole, trying to coax the creature out. He engaged himself in making magic potions and reciting a variety of spells.

"Jesus, passing down the highway, viewed the scene taking place beside the snakehole. The snake, emerging from the hole, hailed the saint, 'O Spirit of God, shining candle of all creatures! A mere thirty-year old man is trying to lure me out of my lair, though I am a full three hundred years of age!'

"Jesus listened to the snake's complaint, then took his leave. Subsequently, he revisited the area.

" 'How's the spell-casting going?' he asked the sorcerer.

" 'I've managed to charm the snake into my basket,' he commented.

"Jesus lifted the wicker lid and peered in. There was the snake, all coiled up.

"Jesus, wondering, asked, 'Why did you follow this man and allow yourself to be so easily trapped?' After all you said of yourself, how did you end up in here?'

" 'None of his charms worked to catch me,' replied the snake. 'I might have even bitten him and had the advantage. No, it was his hypnotic repetition of God's Name which mesmerized me, charming me little by little inexorably into this basket. It was the Divine Name which charmed me. I would like to see a hundred souls like me sacrificed in His Name.' "

— 'Attâr, *Mosibat-nâma,*
p.68

28— JESUS AND THE FOOL

"Jesus was running for the hills as if a raging lion were hot on his tail. A friend, encountering him on this mad flight, begged to know: 'What are you running away from? You're darting like a flushed quail, yet there's no one in

"Jesus, ignoring his friend's urgent pleas, only quickened his pace, running all the harder. Undaunted, his friend tagged along breathlessly, up hill and down dale, imploring him to reveal what the trouble was. At last, he made a final exasperated plea: 'For God's sake, hold on! There's nobody behind you, neither human foe nor hungry lion in pursuit! No reason for you to be afraid! Just why are you running on like this?'

" 'Don't interfere with me,' was Jesus's rejoinder. 'I'm trying to get away from a fool!'

" 'But aren't you the Messiah?' pressed the friend, refusing to settle for such an offhand answer, 'the Christ who has healed the blind and the deaf and... ?'

" 'Indeed, I am,' acknowledged Jesus.

" 'And are you not that sovereign, that lordly messenger of the mysteries of the supernatural realm?'

" 'Yes, that I am.'

" 'And the same who chanted litanies above a corpse, causing it to spring to life, like a lion upon its prey?'

" 'That I am.'

" 'Are you not that same Jesus who fashioned birds from clay, then animated them with a breath and sent them soaring to the heavens?'

" 'Yes, I am.'

" 'So, O pure spirit, if such feats lie within your power, whom do you fear? Who is there who would refuse to be your vassal in the world when presented such irrefutable proofs?'

" 'By the exalted Essence of God, I swear,' attested Jesus, 'by all the Attributes of Him Who created the soul before eternity and molded the body to contain it, Who is the cynosure of all the firmament whirling in rapturous worship around Him, its collar torn in ecstasy. I have chanted His Name over a mountain, so that it was cleft in twain, its robe rent from neck to navel. I have raised the dead in His Name and summoned things into existence by invoking it. But when I recited the Name lovingly over the heart of a fool, a hundred thousand times over, it was to no avail.'

" 'My efforts proved useless. In fact, the clay of his heart became rough gravel in which no seed could ever sprout, and his bosom grew as hard as granite.'

" 'But elsewhere,' insisted the friend, 'invocation of the Divine Name stood you in good stead, and you were able to work wonders. How does it happen that in this case it has proven ineffective? Why did this remedy fail here, while it cured infirmities elsewhere?'

"Jesus replied:

" *'The pain of blindness is a tribulation,*
   but to be smitten with stupidity
      is the wrath of God.

" *'Tribulation's infliction stirs compassion.*
   The affliction of stupidity only galls.
      Over the fool's heart rests

" *'The seal of God; no hand may mend it.'*
   So flee from fools, as Jesus fled.
      Alas, the blood shed by the company of
         fools!"

— Rumi, *Mathnawi*,
III, vv. 2570-99

29— JESUS AND THE DISRESPECT OF DISCIPLES

Success in adab[1] *is what*
   we seek from God.
      The discourteous are cast out from Divine
         grace.

1. *Adab* has various meanings, depending on the context; it may be translated as 'rules of behavior', 'etiquette', 'culture', 'civilization', 'literature', 'decorum', 'good manners', or, among the Sufis, 'a code of chivalrous courtesy practised for the sake of cultivating virtue and to discipline the lower soul *(nafs)*'.

Discourtesy does not yourself alone disgrace
but ignites the fires of insolence
on every horizon.

From Paradise, the 'Table Spread'[1] has come
without traffic or trade, or
words spoken or heard.

But among the people of Moses[2]
the vulgar spurned the celestial fare,
demanding, "Where's our lentils and
garlic?"

When heaven's bounty ceased,
they were left with their mattocks
and scythes, toiling in the fields.

Then Jesus pleaded for intercession,
and the fare and bounty on platters
and trays was sent from heaven;

Holding forth their hollow bowls,
the beggars by the wayside
with brazen impudence, asked for more.

"This supply from heaven," Jesus tried to reason,
"stays on earth forever,

---

1. An allusion to the Qoran, *Mâ'edah (The Table Spread)*, 114: "Jesus, son of Mary, said: 'O Lord, send us down a table spread with food from Paradise, that it may be a feast for us, for the first and last among us, and a sign from You. Give us sustenance, for You are the Best of Sustainers.' "

2. An allusion to another instance of Divine sustenance mentioned in the Qoran, *Baqarah (The Cow)*, 57 and 61: "And We caused the white cloud to overshadow you and sent down on you the manna and quails, saying, 'Eat of the good things wherewith We have provided you... And when ye said, 'O Moses! We are weary of one kind of food; so call upon thy Lord for us that He might bring forth for us of that which the earth groweth of its herbs and its cucumbers and its corn and its lentils and its onions. He said, 'Would you exchange what is higher for what is lower? Go down to settled country; there you shall get what you demand.' And humiliation and wretchedness were stamped upon them and they were visited with wrath from God."

non-temporal and immutable.

"To act so suspiciously, showing your gluttony
exposes your thanklessness
at the royal table."

So the gates of plenitude shut, and
before such importunity, such blind greed,
the celestial table disappeared.

Whatever of depression or gloom brfalls you
comes of irreverence and bravado.
Whoever displays discourtesy on the
Beloved's way.

Is a brigand, not a man.
Adab lights the skies up;
adab made the angels blessed and pure.

Whoever is irreverent on the Way
is dazed and plunges
into a chasm of bewilderment.
— Rumi, *Mathnawi,*
I, vv. 78-92

30— JESUS AND THE REVIVAL OF A PILE OF BONES

"A fool fell in with Jesus and told him about a pile of bones which he had seen lying in a gully, asking to be taught the Divine Name invoked for reviving the dead, 'so that I may do a good deed by giving life to those bones.'

"Jesus told him to hold his tongue, saying that he had no business being concerned with such things, as evinced by the way he was speaking, by the very way he breathed. The worthiness of one who performed such works was indicated in the fact that 'his breath must be purer than the falling rain and quicker in action than the angels. Whole lifetimes must

118

be spent till such a breath may come out purified, till one might become worthy of being entrusted with the treasure of the heavens. If you were to be granted Moses's staff in hand, would that make your hand the miraculous limb of Moses?[1]'

" 'Well, if I cannot have this power,' insisted the fool, 'why do you not invoke the Divine Name yourself over those bones?'

"Jesus appealed to the Lord, begging to know how it was that this man was more concerned with reviving a pile of bones than putting life into his own dead self. 'Instead of seeking to liberate his own sick soul, he is preoccupied with that of a stranger!' marveled Jesus.

"The Lord replied, 'Be warned that he who sows thistles in this world will not be seen in the rose garden of the next! Roses turn to thorns in his grasp, and the help which he proffers is that of the viper. This evil-doer is snake's poison itself, the reverse of the virtuous potion he pretends to present you. Avoid him like the plague, for his words and deeds will no more bear fruit than the willow-tree.' "

"The more the foolish companion persisted, the more Jesus realized that he was bent on a career course of aggravation. No counsel would have any effect in deterring him. The more one seeks to advise a fool, the more he thinks one is jealously trying to lead him astray. In the end, Jesus simply gave up and yielded to the youth's plea to invoke the Divine Name over the dead bones.

"And the Almighty decreed that those bones should be assembled for the sake of that simple fellow, and take again the shape of the living being whose frame they had once formed.

"And it so happened that the being in question was a fearsome lion, which promptly leapt up and, with one blow of its mighty paw, split the simpleton's head right open, so that the grey matter popped out like a nut from its shell — or

---

1. Reference is to the glowing hand of Moses, cited in both the Torah (the Old Testament) and the Qoran (A'râf [The Heights], 107 and other places).

that is to say, what there was of it to spill out!

"Jesus, astonished, asked the lion why he had killed the man 'just like that'.

"The lion replied simply: 'He was bothering you.'

"Jesus then asked why the lion had not devoured his prey.

"The latter answered: 'It was not my portion, my daily bread.' "

> *O Disposer of all things*
>   *for us in the world,*
> *Free us from the jibes*
>   *and the conflict of it all!*
> *You set before us sustenance,*
>   *but only as a snare;*
> *Show us everything*
>   *as it really is!*

"The lion told Jesus: 'This game was not mine to consume. If I were entitled to a share in this life, I would be living still. If I were to concern myself with those already dead, I would be like the donkey who, on arriving at a clear running stream, instead of drinking from it, plants his feet in it and urinates. When eternal life is at hand, as it is when one encounters a prophet, only fools would behave in such a foolish way when the water of life is accessible to them. Instead of concerning themselves with a dead thing like a body, they should be crying to be brought to true life at the hands of one who is a vehicle for the Divine Command of 'Be!' "[1]

— Rumi, *Mathanawi,*
II, vv. 141-155 and 457-473

This same tale is told by 'Attâr in the *Elâhi-nâma* (p.91) with minor variation in the narrative detail.

1. This suggests the reference in both Torah (Old Testament) and Qoran to the command of God, "Be! and it was," through which Jesus, as a prophet and Perfect Man, was able to bring the dead to life. Here, of course, it is not the dead body, but the dead soul, which is in need of that reviving force.

31— THE VIRTUE OF BEING INOFFENSIVE

Just because you hold the sword,
a man should not be killed —
nothing is unremembered in God's eyes.

The swordblade was not fashioned for oppression
or villainy, nor grapes
for the wine-press harvested.

Jesus by the wayside saw a body slain,
tossed aside; he touched his finger
to his lips in wonder.

"Who did you kill," he asked, "for you so basely
to be slain? And who will kill
the killer who killed you?"

Do not raise your hand to cause someone pain,
lest you find a fist
to bring you greater pain.
        — Nâser Khosrow, *Diwân,*
        vol. I, p.519

32— JESUS RAISING THE DEAD FOR A FOOL

"It is related that once while Jesus was walking through a graveyard, he paused and prayed, entreating, 'O Lord, by Your favor and grace, revive one of the dead for me!' At once the earth erupted, and a tall figure rose up from the ground, coming to stand before him.

" 'Who are you?' Jesus hailed him.

"The apparition gave a name.

" 'And when did you die?'

" 'Two thousand seven hundred years ago.'

" 'How does it feel to be dead?'

" 'The bitter taste of death is still with me.'

" 'What did God do to make death so unsavory for you?'

" 'Ever since I died, I have been subjected to an unremitting interrogation over the half share of an orphan's property which I retained for myself, and I have yet to be acquitted for this matter.'

"So saying, he lay back in his grave."

— Ansâri, *Tafsir-e 'erfâni,*
vol. I, p.183

The same story is told by 'Attâr in the *Elâhi-hâma* (p.237) with miror variations, concluding with a lengthy moral condemning the sin of avarice.

33— JESUS RAISES A DEAD MAN

"Jesus, son of Mary, was passing by a cemetery, when he stopped and went over to call a man up from the dead, raised by God's command. He then asked him who he was. 'I was a porter,' the man replied, 'carrying loads for people. One day, when I was carrying kindling for someone, I happened to break off a piece with which to pick my teeth. Ever since I died, I have been held to account for that act.' "

— Qoshairi, *op. cit.,* p.291

34— JESUS AND THE THIEF

"It is related of Christ that once, upon encountering a man who was engaged in thievery, he asked if the man was stealing. 'I swear by the Name of Him than Whom there is no other God,' he cried. 'O Jesus, in God's Name, I am not stealing!' Jesus commented, 'You have told the truth and my eyes has lied.' " — 'Ebâdi, *Tasfiyah fi ahwâl at-tasawwofah,* p.62.

35— JESUS AND THE PROSTITUTE

"Jesus was seen to be leaving the home of a woman of ill repute, and was hailed, 'O Spirit of God! That is no place for you. How have you come to fall into a state where you have to visit such a house?'

"Jesus replied, 'Unable to sleep last night, I rose to go to the mount to commune with God. The way to the mountain became veiled for me and, in groping my way, I found myself at this house, which belonged, I became aware, to a woman who was ill-famed amongst the Israelites.'

"As soon as the woman saw Jesus, she realized that he had not come without purpose. She rose forthwith and came to him, falling at his feet with a weeping and lamentation. Repenting of her past, she saw the light.

"It was revealed to Jesus that, in the words of the Lord: 'We desired that you bring this woman into the circle of Our friends. For this reason We obscured the way for you.' " — Ansâri, *op, cit.,* vol. I, p.473

36— JESUS AND THE WORSHIPPERS OF GOD

"It is recorded that Jesus came upon a group of people who were busy with worship and pious observance. He asked them why they were so engaged in all this pious activity. They replied, 'We fear the fire of hell.' 'Then you are a cowardly people,' was Jesus's remark.

"Another group farther along were even more fervent in their passionate ritual observance. Posing the same question, he was given the reply: 'In the hope of reaching heaven.' He rejoined, 'Why do you not place your hopes in God himself? Who is it, then, who has bestowed all these bounties upon you?' "

— *Ibid,* vol. II., p.237

37— JESUS AND THE WORSHIPPERS

"Jesus encountered a group of worshippers of God, who were completely immersed in their practice, maintaining that they both feared hell-fire and aspired to heavenly bliss. 'How strange!' observed Jesus. 'You are afraid of something created and you place your hopes in something else which is created.'

"Then he came upon another group, who were

worshipping God out of love for Him. Jesus remarked, 'You are truly the friends of God. God has commanded me to be friends with you, to be with you and to sit with you.' "
— *Ibid,* p.402

38— JESUS'S REQUEST FOR THE TABLE SPREAD[1]

"When Jesus prayed for a laden table to be sent down from the Lord, his supplication was answered and such a festive board was provided. However, the Lord said, 'While I am perfectly ready to feed those who seek to eat, but I have friends who go hungry and observe patient constancy and forebearance, seeking nothing of Me but Me and finding solace only in remembrance of Me, through My Compassion avoiding self-concern and through My Love gazing at no one but Me.' " — *Ibid,* vol. I, p.270

39— JESUS'S LIFE OF WANDERING

"It is written that Jesus, son of Mary, never settled down and was forever wandering from place to place. When asked why, he replied, 'Perhaps I might set foot one day where a saint has trod and, stepping in his tracks, find intercession from sins.' " — *Ibid,* vol. II, p. 646

40— JESUS AND THE WASHERMAN

"They have written that one day Jesus came upon a washerman and, on looking at him, saw, through his miraculous insight, the man's fate poised over his head, with its face turned towards the man.

"Jesus warned, 'This man is going to pass from this world within the hour. Prepare yourselves for the funeral rites.'

"The washerman went away. The hour passed, and he returned, still alive.

"Jesus's companions addressed him, 'O messenger of God, the hour has passed and the washerman is still alive!'

1. Reference is to *Mâ'edah (The Table Spread).* 114

"Jesus turned to the man and asked him, 'What happened to you during this hour?'

He replied, 'I saw two hungry paupers along the way, and as I chanced to have two loaves with me, I gave them to the two men.'

" 'Then what did you see?' asked Jesus.

" 'I found a black snake in my backpack, and as it wriggled out, I noticed that it had a muzzle bound firmly round its jaws, holding its mouth tightly shut!' "[1]

— *Ibid,* vol. I, p.504

---

1. 'Poised fate' (*qaḍhâ-ye taʿliqi* or *moʿallaq*) is one which has been foreordained; however, as it has yet to be carried out, it may, by means of repentance, prayer, alms or other virtuous acts, be forestalled.

SELECTED BIBLIOGRAPHY

Note: The initials AHS after a publication
date indicate the Iranian solar year,
reckoned from the Hegira.

Abu Bakr Mohammad ebn 'Abdo'l-Karim, *Ferdaus al-morshediyah fi asrâr as-samadiyah* (Persian alternate title: *Sirat-nâma-ye shaikh abu eshâq Kâzeruni),* trans. (Arabic to Persian) Mahmud ebn 'Othmân (Kazerun, Iran, d. 728/1327), ed. Fritz Meier, Istanbul, 1943; ed. Iraj Afshâr, Tehran, 1333 AHS/1954

Aflâki, Shamso'd-Din Ahmad, *Manâqeb al-'ârefin,* 2 vols., Ankara, 1959-61. (in Persian)

Ansâri, Khwâja 'Abdo'llâh, *Tafsir-e 'erfâni wa adabi-ye qor'ân-e majid,* ed. Habibo'llâh Âmuzegâr, Tehran, 1348 AHS/1969

Anwâr, Shâh Qâsem, *Diwân,* ed. Sa'id Nafisi, Tehran, 1337 AHS/1958

Arberry, A.J. *Discourses of Rumi,* London, 1961. (English translation of Rumi, Maulânâ Jalâlo'd-Din, *Fihe mâ fihe)*

— *The Doctrine of the Sufis,* Cambridge, 1977 (English partial translation of Kalâbâdhi, Abu Bakr Mohammad, *Ta'arrof li-madhhab ahl at-tasawwof)*

— *Muslim Saints and Mystics,* London and Boston, 1976. (Translation of excerpts from 'Attâr, Farido'd-Din, *Tadhkerat al-auliyâ')*

'Attâr, Shaikh Farido'd-Din, *Diwân-e qasâ'ed wa tarji'ât wa ghazaliyât,* ed. Sa'id Nafisi, Tehran, 1339 AHS/1960

— *Elâhi-nâma,* ed. Helmut Ritter, Tehran, 1359 AHS/1980

— *Mosibat-nâma,* ed. Nurâni Wesâl, Tehran, 1356 AHS/1977

— *Manteq at-tair,* ed. Seyyed Sâdeq Gauharin, Tehran, 1356 AHS/1977. (English translation: Noth, G.S., *The Conference of the Birds* [1954], Berkeley, Calif. [paperback], 1971.)

— *Oshtor-nâma,* ed. Mahdi Mohaqqeq, Tehran, 1339 AHS/1960

— *Tadhkerat al-auliyâ',* ed. Mohammad Este'lami, Tehran, 1354 AHS/1975

Auhadi Marâghi Esfahâni, *Diwân,* ed. A.S. Usha, Madras, 1951.

Baqli, Shaikh Ruzbehân, *'Abhar al-'âsheqin,* ed. J. Nurbakhsh, Tehran, 1349 AHS/1970

— *Ruzbehân-nâma,* selected works of the saint, ed. Mohammad Taqi Dâneshpazhuh, Tehran, 1347 AHS/1968

— *Sharh-e shathiyât,* ed. Henry Corbin, Tehran, 1360 AHS/1981.

Bâkhzari, Abo'l-Mofâkher, *Aurâd al-ahbâb wa fosus al-âdâb,* ed. Iraj Afshâr, Tehran, 1358 AHS/1979 (in Persian)

Bertels, Yevgeni Edvardovich, *Tasawwof wa adabiyât-e tasawwof,* (Persian translation of the Russian) Sirus Izadi, Tehran, 1356 AHS/1977. (This work includes the text of the calligraphic MS. of the Persian-language anonymous glossary of Sufi terminology, the *Mer'ât-e 'oshâq,* discovered by Prof. Bertels in the archives of the former Asiatic Museum of Leningrad.)

Bokhârâ'i, Abu Ebrâhim Esmâ'il ebn Mohammad, *Sharh-e ta'arrof,* 4 vols., Lucknow, 1330/1912. (The writer of the abridgement of this Persian paraphrase of Kalâbâdhi's work (see listing under Kalâbâdhi) is unknown; it is published under the title: *Kholâsa-ye sharh-e ta'arrof* Tehran, 1349 AHS/1970.)

'Ebâdi, Mansur ebn Ardeshir, *Tasfiyah fi ahwâl at-tasawwofah,* ed. Gholâm-Hosain Yusefi, Tehran, 1343 AHS/1964

'Erâqi, Fakhro'd-Din Ebrâhim, *Resâla-ye lama'ât wa resâla-ye estelâhât,* ed. J. Nurbakhsh, Tehran, 1353

AHS/1974. (see also listing under 'Irâqi for the English translation.)

Ghazâli, Abu Hâmed Mohammad, *Ehyâ al-'olum ad-din,* ed. Zaino'd-Din Abo'l-Fadhl 'Abdo'r-Rahim ebn Hosain al-'Erâqi, 5 vols., Beirut, n. d.; and 4 vols., Bulaq, 1280/1872-73. Persian translation (to which page indications in the footnotes to the text refer): *Ehyâ-ye 'olum-e din,* trans. Mo'ayyedo'd-Din Mohammad Khwârazmi (begun 620/1222, Delhi), ed. Hosain Khadiw Jam, Tehran, 1359 AHS/1981

Ghazâli, Ahmad, *Resâla'i dar mau'eza* (from the collection *Resâla-ye sawâneh wa resâla'i dar mau'eza),* ed. J. Nurbakhsh, Tehran, 1352 AHS/1974

Gibb, H.A.R., and J.H. Kramers, editors, *The Shorter Encyclopedia of Islam,* Leiden, 1974

Hâfez, Shamso'd-Din Mohammad, *Diwân:* (Perhaps the most definitive from the point of view of research and erudition is the work by Farzâd, Mas'ud, *Hâfez: gozâreshi az nima râh,* 1352 AHS/1973) *Diwân,* ed. Qazwini, Mohammad, and Ghâni, Qâsem, 1320 AHS/1941

Hamadhâni, 'Aino'l-Qodhât, *Nâmahâ-ye 'aino'l-qodhât hamadhâni,* ed. 'Ali Naqi Manzawi and 'Afif 'Osairân, Tehran, 1350 AHS/1969

— *Tamhidât,* ed. 'Afif 'Osairan, Tehran, 1341. AHS/1962

Hedâyat, Redha Qoli, *Riyâdh al-'ârefin,* Tehran, 1316 AHS/1937

Hojwiri, 'Ali ebn 'Othmân, *Kashf al-mahjub,* ed. V.A. Zhukovskiy, Leningrad, 1926. English translation (from an incomplete MS.) under the original title: trans. R.A. Nicholson, London, 1976 (latest reprint)

'Irâqi, Fakhruddin, *Divine Flashes,* trans. W.C. Chittick and P.L. Wilson, London, 1982. (For the original Persian text, see listing under 'Erâqi.)

Kalâbâdhi, Abu Bakr Mohammad, *Ta'arrof li-madhhab ahl at-tasawwof,* ed. A.J. Arberry, Cairo, 1934. (For the English translation, see listing under Arberry.)

Kâshâni, 'Ezzo'd-Din Mahmud, *Mesbâh al-hedâyah wa*

meftâh al-kefâyah, ed. Jalâlo'd-Din Homâ'i, Tehran, 1325 AHS/1946. (This is a 17th/13th-century Persian revision of the Arabic text of Sohrawardi, Shehâbo'd-Din Abu Hafs 'Omar, *'Awâref al-ma'âref.)*

Khosrau, Nâser: See listing under Qobâdiyâni.

Lâhiji, Shaikh Shamso'd-Din Mohammad, *Sharh-e golshan-e râz,* ed. Kaiwân Sami'i, Tehran, 1337 AHS/1958

Mer'ât-e 'oshâq: See listing under Bertels.

Nezâmi, Hakim Abu Mohammad Elyâs ebn Yusef, *Makhzan al-asrâr,* in the collection *Kolliyât-e khamsa,* Tehran, 1351. AHS/1972

Nurbakhsh, Javad, *Sufism: Fear and Hope, Contraction and Expansion, Gathering and Dispersion, Intoxication and Sobriety, Annihilation and Subsistence,* New York, 1982

— *Sufism: Meaning, Knowledge and Unity,* New York, 1981.

— *What the Sufis Say,* New York, 1980

Qobâdiyâni, Nâser Khosrau, *Diwân* (along with the *Roshanâ'i-nâma, Sa'âdat-nâma* and a prose treatise), ed. Nasro'llâh Taqawi, Tehran, 1307 AHS/1928

Qoshairi, Abo'l-Qâsem, *Resâla-ye qoshairiya* (Persian translation of the Arabic original by an anonymous disciple, ed. Badi'oz-Zamân Foruzânfar, Tehran, (published 1340 AHS/1961) (reprinted) 1361. AHS/1982

Râzi, Najmo'd-Din, *Marmuzât asadi dar mazmurât-e dâ'udi,* ed. Mohammad Redhâ Shafi'i Kadkani, Tehran, 1352 AHS/1973

— *Mersâd al-ebâd,* ed. Mohammmad Amin Riyâhi, Tehran, 1352 AHS/1973

Rumi, Maulânâ Jalâlo'd-Din, *Diwân-e kabir yâ kolliyât-e shams,* 10 vols., ed. Badi'oz-Zamân Foruzânfar, 1336 AHS/1959

— *Fihe mâ fihe,* ed. 'Abdo'l-Majid Daryâbâdi, Azamgarh(India),1928; and ed.Badi'oz-zamân Foruzânfar, Tehran, 1342 AHS/1962. (For the English translation see listing under Arberry.)

— *Mathnawi-ye ma'nawi,* ed. R.A. Nicholson, Tehran. 1356 AHS/1977 (fourth printing). English translation under the title of *The Mathnawi of Jalalu'ddin Rumi,* 8 vols., ed., trans. and comm. R.A. Nicholson, London, 1925-40; 1977 (fourth printing; 3 vols., paperback). (The London paperback edition represents the first three volumes of the initial E.J.W. Gibb Memorial publication, namely, the English translation; the Tehran edition represents vols. IV through VI of the initial publication, namely, the original Persian text as edited by Nicholson; the final two volumes of the first edition are Nicholson's commentary.)

Sa'di, Shaikh Maslahod-Din, *Golestân,* ed. Khalil Khatib-Rahbar, Tehran, 1348 AHS/1969

— *Qasâ'ed,* included in the poet's collected works, *Kolliyât-e shaikh sa'di,* ed. Mohammad 'Ali Forughi, Tehran, 1338 AHS/1959

Sanâ'i, Hakim Abo'l-Majd Majdud, *Diwân,* ed. Modarres Radhawi, Tehran, 1354 AHS/1975

— *Hadiqat al-haqiqat wa shari'at at-tariqat,* ed. Modarres Radhawi, Tehran, 1329 AHS/1950. English partial translation: *The First Book of the Hadiqatu'l-Haqiqat or the Enclosed Garden of the Truth of the Hakim Sanâ'i of Ghazna,* ed. and trans. Major J. Stephenson (1908), (fourth impression) New York, 1975.

Schimmel, Annemarie, *Mystical Dimensions of Islam,* Chapel Hill (No. Car., USA), 1975

Shabestari, Shaikh Mahmud, *Golshan-e râz,* ed. J. Nurbakhsh, Tehran, 1355 AHS/1976. English translations: *The Rose-Garden of Mysteries,* ed. and trans. Edward Henry Whinfield, London, 1880; and *The Secret Garden,* trans. Juraj Paska, New York and London, 1969

Shirâzi, Mohammad Ma'sum, Nâ'ebo's-Sadr (Ma'sum 'Ali Shâh), *Tarâ'eq al-haqâ'eq,* ed., Mohammad Ja'far Mahjub, 3 vols., 1339-45 AHS/1960-66

Sohrawardi, Shehâbo'd-Din Abu Hafs 'Omar, *'Awâref al-ma'âref,* Bulaq (Egypt), 1289/1872-73 (in the margin of Ghazâli, Abu Hâmed Mohammad, *Ehyâ' al-'olum ad-din).* English partial translation under the original title by Clarke, Wilberforce, Calcutta, 1891; New York, 1970. For the Persian revision see the listing under Kâshâni.)

Solami, Abu 'Abdo'r-Raḥmân, *Jawâme' âdâb aṣ-ṣufiyah* and *'Oyub an-nafs wa modâwâtohâ,* ed. Etan Kohlberg, Jerusalem, 1976

Ṭabasi, Darwish Moḥammad, *Âthâr-e darwish moḥammad ṭabasi,* ed. Iraj Afshâr and Moḥammad Taqi Dâneshpazhuh, Tehran, 1351 AHS/1972

Tahânawi, Moḥammad A'lâ ebn 'Ali, *Kashshâf estelâhât al-fonun,* 2 vols., ed. Asiatic Society of Bengal,